SCUBA DIVING SAFETY

C. W. DUEKER, M.D.

WORLD

World Publications
Mountain View, California

Library of Congress Cataloging in Publication Data

Dueker, Christopher Wayne, 1929–
    Scuba diving safety.

    1. Scuba diving–Safety measures. I. Title.
GV840.S78D83   797.2'3   78-55789
ISBN 0-89037-135-0

World Publications
Mountain View, CA

For Joyce

*Therefore a man leaves his father and his mother and cleaves
to his wife, and they become one flesh.*

Genesis 2:24 RSV

Table of Contents

The Challenge

There is something in man that wants to test limits
But nature limits set that cannot be over reached;
For to go beyond the bounds of what is set by more than man
Is to experience the discipline of a real, unseen hand,
And so, to know that there are limits kindly set,
Man, who is yet man, can bend and know the challenge is not
Always to see how high or how deep but to know the bounds.
—Joyce Dueker

Introduction

Toward Safer Diving

How dangerous is diving? Obviously there is no simple answer. Certain types of diving, such as North Sea oil work, are very dangerous. But recreational diving isn't very dangerous, if practiced properly. This distinguishes it from sports that are dangerous under the best of circumstances. Divers, in a way, are to blame for the image of diving as a hazardous activity. In its early days, diving was known as a challenging, death-defying sport for only the bravest, strongest men. Movies talked of underwater pressures that "crushed heads like they were melons." The truth about diving safely gradually became known and diving is recognized today as an enjoyable sport suitable for a wide variety of people.

Unfortunately, there are still too many accidents in recreational diving. Despite good equipment and training programs, diving can be considered hazardous. Any active sport will have accidents, but diving accident reports reveal that most accidents could have been prevented by proper diving. Many of the fatalities could have been prevented by proper attention to rescue and resuscitation techniques.

Safe diving does not make diving less fun. On the contrary, the safe diver can have more fun because he is not worried about a possible disaster. Diving safety requires attention to diver selection, diver training, and post certification diving techniques.

Diver Selection

Some people employed in the diving industry are concerned that diving doesn't have the mass appeal of tennis and jogging. The average diver usually doesn't care how popular his sport is. A few want to be doing the "right thing" but most prize exclusiveness and don't want to share their favorite diving sites. Actually, all divers have benefited from diving's increased popularity. The

1

introduction of new equipment and development of diving facilities in exotic places depend on a large market.

But promoting diving as the sport for everyone is unwise and dishonest. Most people can participate in some form of sport for recreation or fitness. Because a certified diver is officially qualified for unrestricted open water diving, the sport should be reserved for the physically and mentally fit. The challenges of diving come from its nature as a vigorous sport undertaken in a potentially hostile environment. Basically, a diver must be able to withstand unfriendly seas and the problems associated with pressure changes.

Most instructors require their students to have a medical clearance. This is the simplest method of diver selection but the least valuable. As will be discussed later, there are certain physical requirements that must not be ignored. But most potential students can pass a physical.

The instructor's evaluation of a student's emotional stability is much more important. This evaluation begins with a pre-enrollment interview discussing reasons a person wants to dive, past experiences in the ocean, expectations, fears, and such. The evaluation continues throughout the class in an effort to avoid certification of emotionally unqualified persons.

The most common weakness in student selection is the failure to require basic swimming ability. The new equipment really does not make diving safe for non-swimmers and the standard scuba course is not long enough for both swimming instruction and scuba training. Students should master basic water skills before starting to learn how to dive.

Training

Training has come a long way, but improvements are still needed. Slightly more than ten percent of diving fatalities occur during instruction. A review of the instruction fatalities show problems during deep dives, separation from partners, and hazardous skill training.

Diving is fun. But diving classes also have to teach subjects like diving illnesses because divers need to know how to take care of themselves. Sometimes an emphasis on safety training results in classes that resemble medical school lectures. This is unnecessary and more confusing than helpful. The average diving student needs accurate basic information on safety training, not treatises on physiology and pathophysiology. Diving maladies are real, and students should not be told that these things will never happen to them. Two areas of particular concern are the use of decompression tables and the risks of deep diving. These should be discussed in detail before the check out dive.

The transition from pool to ocean is a particularly difficult experience for many. New problems of buoyancy, surf, currents, rocks, kelp, poor visibility, and cold bother many students. The conscientious instructor carefully evaluates each student before allowing graduation from pool work. During the check out dive, no one should be allowed to wander off. A surprising number of accidents occur when a student decides to quit the dive and the instructor allows him to return to shore alone.

The ocean check out dive is not just a fun dive. Students begin to learn how to evaluate sea conditions and to tell when diving is unwise. They also learn how to evaluate themselves by learning that on certain days their physical and emotional condition may not be suitable for safe diving.

Because a lot of diving is done in remote areas, divers cannot rely on lifeguards or rescue squads. Each diver needs to know basic rescue and resuscitation skills. Instructors may not be qualified to teach resuscitation but they can introduce the subject and stress its importance. Ocean check outs provide an opportunity to practice emergency accident management. Each student should learn the importance of staying near his buddy.

Post Certification Diving

The newly certified diver is still a beginner. New divers should be encouraged to take advanced courses to improve their skills and they should consider club diving programs. But, even experienced divers have serious accidents. These accidents usually result from forgetting or ignoring safe diving principles. When diving clubs have contests to see who can use the most tanks in a day, you start to wonder if there is any hope for safer diving.

Consider your own diving practice. A checklist for safe diving follows. A safe diver should:

a. plan each diving day with safety in mind
b. dive only when in good health
c. keep equipment well maintained
d. evaluate the sea before entering it
e. keep records of dive depths and times

f. avoid deep dives

g. quit before being chilled

h. always dive with another trained person

i. know how to use your equipment and buddy's equipment

j. surface before running out of air

k. avoid overexertion

l. know the warning signs of impending panic

m.use safe diving technique such as no breathholding ascents, no skip breathing

n. know how to rescue and treat an injured diver

o. follow other safe diving rules

Learning never stops for the sensible diver. Clubs and classes provide opportunities for more specialized training and reviews of standard skills. Diving should not be a particularly dangerous sport. It is enjoyed by many people who would never climb rock faces or jump from airplanes. It becomes dangerous when divers ignore the risks associated with an alien underwater environment. The goal is to make safety an integral, natural part of all diving. Divers should be introduced to safe diving practices as beginning students and continue these practices throughout their diving careers.

1

Sensible Diving

"Candidates beyond the age of thirty years shall not be considered for initial training in diving . . ." Manual of the Medical Department, U.S. Navy.

"Today virtually anyone can learn to be a diver. With modern equipment you don't have to be an expert swimmer." Paraphrase from a diving school advertisement.

The truth of eligibility for diving lies between the Navy's rigid standards and the enroll-at-any-cost philosophy of some diving schools. Many people can enjoy safe diving but, because the sport is a vigorous one practiced in remote waters under increased atmospheric pressure, not *everyone* can participate. Divers must be capable of meeting challenges arising from rough water, planned or unplanned long swims, cold water, and dark areas containing a variety of rocks, plants, and animals. Other challenges include the use of new equipment, interaction with a buddy, the direct effects of pressure (squeeze and overexpansion), the indirect effects of pressure (narcosis and decompression sickness), air supply management, planning dives, and personal management of accidents.

THE MAKING OF A DIVER

Fitness for diving then requires good physical and emotional health. Health changes with time, so fitness may vary from day to day. The simplest method of determining who can dive is to establish a list of qualifying standards. But these standards may have little value in actually promoting safe diving. For example, Navy physical requirements are unnecessarily restrictive for recreational divers. They work reasonably well in screening large groups of candidates for jobs involving diving at anytime in adverse, hazardous conditions. At the same time, Navy standards provide virtually no guidance to the extremely important matter of emotional health. There is no perfect way to select diving candidates. Despite many attempts, no way exists to reliably determine who will be an effective, safe diver.

In recreational diving each person can be considered individually. As will be discussed, there are a few firm requirements for students. Beyond these there is a wide area for evaluation by student, physician, and instructor.

Diver selection begins with the applicant's self-evaluation. Can you walk, run, swim, and climb? Are there any limitations in your activity? The next step is to talk to an instructor who may ask a few basic fitness questions. A physician's examination including your total medical history and a physical examination should complete the preparation. Some diving instructors do not require a physician's evaluation of their potential students. Justification for this oversight is that the examination of apparently healthy persons yields few disqualifying results. A misinterpretation of national diving fatality statistics perpetuates this philosophy. Autopsies suggest that only 12 percent were caused by medical conditions detectable by medical evaluation. This may not include all contributory causes to the accident. For example, a diver with a history of leg cramps develops a leg cramp, panics then drowns. Furthermore, this retrospective type of investigation does not record the number of potential students who failed to pass medical exams and never enrolled in scuba classes. A medical examination is not difficult to obtain and can be very important. Instructors who do not require their classes to visit a physician are putting their students and themselves at risk.

Emotional Health

Emotional stability is essential for safe diving. Unstable persons react unpredictably when stressed and their behavior may endanger them and their companions. A significant proportion of diving's challenges are mental, rather than physical. The emotions, too, affect physical capacity. Some specific mental traits include: attitude toward diving, calmness under stress, resourcefulness or ingenuity, claustrophobia, and spirit of cooperation.

Mental health is much more difficult to evaluate than physical health. The physician may elicit a history suggestive of emotional instability, but most of the evaluation will depend on the instructor's observations during class sessions. Hints come from a student's behavior in lectures and during pool work. A student who appears unduly apprehensive or inappropriately bold needs special watching. No student should be forced along through a course.

Often ineptness serves as a cover for anxiety. One student continually had equipment problems in class. He came to the ocean check out dive wearing the same weights he had used for scuba in a fresh water pool without a wet suit. Not surprisingly, he had problems getting down. After the third dive he began hyperventilating and had passed out before the instructor could reach him. Fortunately, there was no way he could have sunk. The instructor now pays more attention to the signals given by students in the pool. He doesn't take anyone to the ocean until he and the student both feel ready.

Instructors must also evaluate a student's tendency to take chances and be accident prone. These patterns are largely consistent from pool to ocean. The student who disobeys pool rules may well ignore the buddy system, decompression limits, and the threat of narcosis. The student for whom things go wrong repeatedly needs special watching. Accident-proneness is probably a manifestation of emotional instability.

Physical Health

General health is the primary consideration. Divers in good health are less likely to get into trouble and have a better ability to get out of dangerous situations. The diver must be capable of vigorous exercise over an indefinite period of time. A dive planned to be short and simple may be changed by currents, condition of the sea, or equipment failure. Nothing looks sillier than a diver exhausted from having to swim 200 yards back to a boat because of a navigational error.

The following is a discussion of some specific physical considerations. This is not an all-inclusive list, nor is it intended to substitute for a physical examination.

Age. No firm guidelines are necessary for recreational diving. Lower limits depend on strength, coordination, and maturity. Upper limits depend on vigorous health.

Weight. Overweight divers more frequently get decompression sickness. Obese people generally have reduced exercise tolerance.

Eyes, Ears, Nose, and Throat. Vision that can be corrected with glasses or contact lenses is satisfactory for recreational diving. Limited underwater visibility forces function by feel so that visual handicaps are not usually a problem.

Pressure changes affect mainly the ears and sinuses. *(See chapters on barotrauma.)* Mechanical, allergic, or infectious obstruction of sinus openings or the eustachian tubes will increase the risk of "squeeze." Perforated ear drums may lead to ear infections or dizziness. A history of trauma or surgery in the middle or inner ear needs special evaluation since further pressure exposure may cause a reoccurrence of the defect. External ear infections should be treated before diving is permitted.

For scuba diving a normal bite is needed to grip the mouth piece. One Canadian military diver choked to death on his displaced dentures.

Respiratory System. Normal pulmonary function is essential because of the need for heavy exertion and to minimize the likelihood of lung rupture. Evaluation includes history, examination, and chest X-ray. Childhood asthma with no evidence of permanent damage and no current activity impairment does not make diving dangerous. Active asthma or emphysema may reduce exercise capacity and increase chances of rupture. Very thorough examination is necessary with a history of serious lung disease as these can leave symptomless cysts, scars and bullae.

Not infrequently, people have spontaneous collapse of one lung (pneumothorax) that resolves with treatment. No one can be sure if this collapse will happen again, but the risk in diving makes taking a chance unwise unless surgery has been done to correct an isolated defect. An Air Force pilot was once given special permission to fly despite a spontaneous pneumothorax in his medical past history. On one flight, cabin pressure control failed and pressure suddenly fell from 8,000 to 1,400 feet. (This is a smaller pressure change than encountered in ascending to the surface from thirty feet.) The pilot had chest pain and shortness of breath and had to make an emergency landing. A chest X-ray showed recurrent pneumothorax.

Cardiovascular. The heart and peripheral circulatory system must work perfectly for a diver to be safe. Any congenital or acquired defect that limits activity makes diving unwise. Coronary artery disease limits exertion and may cause dangerous arrhythmia. Heart attacks have become a serious problem in middle aged divers. Many physicians insist that middle aged candidates have stress electrocardiograms before beginning a diving program. High blood pressure results from a variety of circulatory malfunctions. Frequently, the underlying problem limits activity or predisposes to heart malfunction. Mild, uncomplicated hypertension may be all right in diving, but this requires careful consideration.

Gastrointestinal. Abdominal problem areas include diseases such as ulcers, ileitis, and colitis which may be disastrous under stress. These maladies may require medical treatment unavailable in remote areas.

Neuromuscular. Diving requires strength and coordination for propulsion and management of equipment. This doesn't mean that only polished athletes should dive, but a person who gets exhausted lifting a tank needs remedial work before ocean diving.

Central Nervous System. Diving is unsafe for anyone with a central nervous system disease affecting consciousness. A loss of consciousness in the water is obviously very dangerous. Any history of head trauma should be carefully checked.

Virtually all authorities advise against diving for persons with seizure disorders (epilepsy). Some seizure patterns are aggravated by stress or by the elevated carbon dioxide that sometimes occur. Seizures underwater are hazardous. Unfortunately, even people who appear well controlled can have seizures when diving.

Endocrine. Diseases of the endocrine system are disqualifying only when the disease limits activity, requires constant medical supervision, or are controlled by drugs not suitable for diving. These drugs are discussed in chapter 2.

Diabetes mellitus is a complex disease that may involve several organ systems. It presents a definite risk for diving because of the changes in insulin requirements associated with exercise. Hypoglycemia or hyperglycemia can result. A stable diabetic may be able to manage his disease well enough to make diving permissible. This requires coordination between diver, physician, and dive supervisor. Many authorities recommend that diabetics not dive, but this attitude is sometimes unfairly restrictive. Specific diabetic complications of heart, eyes, or nervous system may make diving unwise, but other diabetics can dive—with strict supervision.

Habits. Overindulgence in alcohol causes many problems. Some of these problems are discussed in chapter 2.

Cigarette smoking affects pulmonary and cardiac function and may affect mental activity. Ideally divers should not smoke, but many do. Smokers need more intensive examination of pulmonary and cardiovascular function than other divers of comparable age.

Women as Divers

"Diving . . . a man's world." This paraphrase of a diving advertisement, only a few years ago, fooled no one. Many women dive competently and safely. Too many popular impressions are based on supposition, however. There is a great deal of interest currently being focused on the subject of women as divers—but there is little solid research in the area and few facts.

Basically, there is no reason why women should not be good divers. They have the necessary strength, coordination, and endurance. Their subcutaneous fat deposits improve buoyancy and protect against chilling.

Experiences of international athletes have largely disproved the old theories of the interaction of the menstrual cycle and physical capacity. Women can dive at any time. Mood changes sometimes may affect suitability, but generalizations are not possible.

The question of diving during pregnancy is of special interest. Again, no intensive research has been done in this area. A few general comments can be made:

a. An obstetrician should be consulted regarding diving.
b. Some obstetricians prefer that their patients avoid jarring and strenuous sports during the early stages of pregnancy when fetal implantation is still proceeding.
c. Hyperbaric oxygen has been reported to have caused fetal damage in laboratory animals. This may have no relationship to the human body, but it should be noted. Pregnant divers should be careful not to need recompression therapy, especially during the first trimester.
d. Divers who are not physically fit may find diving overstrenuous in the late stages of pregnancy.
e. The bulk of a near-term uterus may make rock climbing and surf entries difficult and dangerous.

Handicapped Divers

People with many handicaps have become divers—skin and scuba. They must recognize their handicaps and dive only under supervision. Handicapped divers must remember that the buddy system is not designed to provide this sort of supervision. What would happen if the buddy had an accident while diving with a severely handicapped person?

Within these limitations handicapped persons can profit from the enjoyment of water sports. Diving has been popular for paraplegics and amputees. Water supports the paraplegics' legs and provides an enjoyable way of strengthening the upper body. Amputees dive both with and without prosthetic devices.

Recently diving has been used in the therapy of the emotionally disturbed. It seems to be valuable in some cases. Extra supervision and extreme care are required for these classes.

2

Drugs and Diving

Some divers should just stay away from medicine. The man who got the flu two days after a flu shot had a rather rugged Saturday in the California swells. On Sunday he played it safe and took a predive seasickness pill. That was the first and last time he ever got really sick in the water.

In a broad sense drugs include chemicals taken with the intent of helping (medicines) as well as those taken for amusement or self abuse (alcohol, tobacco, or illicit drugs).

Divers use four main types of drugs:

- Medicines used without any intended relationship to diving.
- Tobacco, alcohol, and illicit drugs.
- Drugs used to make diving possible or more enjoyable.
- Drugs used to prevent or to treat diving maladies.

In evaluating the safety of a drug, both the effects of the drug and the effects of diving must be considered. Drug effects that are tolerable on the surface may be dangerous underwater. Pressure may alter a drug's reaction. Unfortunately, many pressure studies involve only very deep exposures and cannot be applied to scuba diving.

Some medicines are in themselves harmless, but are used for illnesses that make diving inadvisable. A diver taking penicillin for pneumonia, for example, should not be diving because of the dangers of pneumonia, not because of the penicillin. A person with heart disease may use drugs which in themselves pose no hazard, but the heart disease itself makes diving unwise. Tranquilizers or other sedatives, narcotics, or drugs such as amphetamines may alter perception and diminish responsiveness to diving challenges. The diver has diminished awareness, unrealistic impressions of situations, and impaired ability to act. Antihistamines used for allergies and sedatives used for blood pressure control can serve as examples. The diver may be unaware of the sedative properties of these drugs. However, when combined with a little narcosis, their effects become dangerously apparent. Narcotics alter mental functions and may obscure warning pain from diving accidents. The early warning pain of decompression sickness may not be noticed by the drugged diver.

Amphetamines have been tested in rats at 198 feet. Behavioral disturbances exceeded those seen with either amphetamines alone or at equivalent pressures without amphetamines.

Many divers smoke, but this does not prove its advisability. The world is continually exposed to evidence that smoking damages the lungs and the circulatory system. Obviously, chronic lung diseases such as emphysema have no place in safe diving. Heavy smoking causes damage to the heart and the blood vessels. Large quantities of nicotine affect mental function by stimulating the nervous system. Smokers have trouble eliminating their respiratory tract secretions. Accumulations of these secretions can make equalizing ears and sinuses difficult.

Alcohol should never be used before a dive. People use it to "feel good" and "relax" without realizing that even very small amounts of alcohol depress the central nervous system. This leads to inattentiveness, carelessness, and impaired muscular coordination. The excitement often seen after drinking results from depression of the higher centers of the brain. Quantities of alcohol that cause no apparent problems on land may be dangerous underwater because the margin for error is so small in diving. Alcohol can also add to the effects of cold, fatigue, seasickness, and nitrogen narcosis.

Larger quantities of alcohol reduce cold water tolerance because alcohol dilates the blood vessels under the skin. This offsets the vessel constriction that normally slows heat loss from the body.

Divers who drink heavily before diving appear to have a greater chance of getting decompression sickness. It is not known whether alcohol increases decompression sickness by promoting careless diving, or if its action on blood vessels somehow causes increased nitrogen uptake by the normally poorly perfused tissues. The answers are not known, largely because most divers do not drink heavily *before* a dive.

Alcohol increases the likelihood that rough water will cause nausea and vomiting. These are obviously dangerous in diving.

A common "first aid" for decompression sickness has been large quantities of whiskey. Many times this so sedates the victim that he does not care about obtaining proper therapy. Minor symptoms may progress to major ones without the diver's awareness.

Illicit drug use, in simple terms, has no place in diving. The action of medically used sedatives, stimulants, and narcotics has been discussed. There are no scientific investigations of how abused drugs act underwater and no studies will likely be done. It requires no fancy study to learn that being stoned underwater is dangerous. Anecdotal reports on marijuana suggest that its use makes diving unpleasant.

The most widely used diving drugs are decongestants used to help ear and sinus "clearing." Antihistamines inhibit secretions. Vasoconstrictors shrink blood vessels. Many decongestant drugs contain both antihistamines and vasoconstrictors. These drugs should not be used chronically as they often cause a reverse activity after several days which increases congestion. Stay away from antihistamines because of sedative effects.

Do not take overdoses of vasoconstrictors as they may raise blood pressure and speed the pulse rate. Some cause mental excitement. Inform a physician of your intention to use this type of drug while diving. Also try the drug on a non-diving day before you use it underwater.

Seasickness prevention is sought by many divers who find the gentle, rocking motion of the sea unwelcome. As noted in the introduction of this chapter, many standard remedies do not work. Some preparations cause drowsiness. As with decongestants, consult a physician and always try out the drug on land first.

Work continues in the search for medicines to prevent inert gas narcosis, oxygen toxicity, and decompression sickness. No definite advances have been made. Do not be misled by spectacular, but unfounded, stories that wonder drugs are available. Specifically, aspirin does not prevent decompression sickness. In the initial treatment of diving accidents, the only valuable drug is oxygen. Follow-up care may involve several other drugs, but these are for physician prescription only.

3

Panic

The newly certified diver picked a beautiful, calm day for his first dive since graduation. He proudly put on his new gear and splashed through a moderate surf. Fifty yards off shore, he dove down. Moments later he surfaced with his mouthpiece dangling and began to gasp and thrash. He made a random grab for his snorkel, then sank. His buddy, in the meantime, was pursuing his own interests. On the beach, an observant instructor interrupted his predive talk to his class and ran into the water. Ideal conditions permitted prompt sighting of the victim who was recovered from fifteen feet and resuscitated quickly. Later, the chagrined diver said he had gotten a mouthful of water and couldn't get enough air. He headed for the surface and that was all he remembered. His regulator and tank functioned normally when checked after the rescue. The stunned class wondered why he had not dumped his weights or inflated his vest. The victim answered, "I never thought of it."

In some ways the old days of "hard hat" diving were more satisfying for accident investigators. Divers died of predictable causes like ruptured air lines, entrapment, blowups, and explosions. A diver who started "acting funny" could be talked to or brought up. The widespread popularity of recreational scuba has changed things. Many of the deaths take place in shallow water with no obvious cause. Even attributing them to air embolism or drowning does not completely satisfy. Why did the diver embolize or drown?

A diver embolized after an emergency ascent, but his tank was half full and the regulator worked fine. Another diver drowned on the surface with a fin caught in some kelp. His fancy knife was not used. Many other examples could be given of divers performing irrationally in response to stress. For a variety of reasons these victims become extremely frightened and act without thinking.

The state of abject terror is called *panic*. Reactions to panic cause many diving accidents. The Oxford Universal Dictionary defines panic as, "A sudden and excessive feeling of alarm or fear . . . and leading to extravagant or injudicious efforts to secure safety."

Dealing with Fear

Fear is almost always part of a dive. Divers must recognize that the sea presents various challenges and there are always possibilities that the challenges cannot be met. In the competent diver this anxiety doesn't cause weeping or incapacitation. It serves to activate the diver to maximum mental and physical alertness. This alerting occurs normally to participants in occupations and hobbies ranging from cardiac surgery to taking final exams. Perhaps this kind of fear should be defined in the Biblical sense as a reverence or respect. Divers should certainly respect the ocean and its power.

The incompetent or novice diver may actually be afraid of the ocean, but not be brave enough to admit it. For a variety of reasons he goes diving, but can hardly be expected to enjoy it. The fearful diver over-reacts to every stress. He makes minor problems important and creates problems when none exist. The sea is full of real and imaginable causes of worry, including cold, darkness, separation from partners, currents and rough seas, buoyancy control, equipment, running out of air, fatigue, entanglement, or plants and animals.

When something goes wrong, the fearful diver becomes extremely anxious and loses all vestiges of rational thought. Behavior control shifts away from the cerebral centers and becomes primitive or instinctive. Instinctive behavior does not always solve problems, especially in the ocean. Three drawbacks that instinctive behavior lead to are breath holding, thoughtless attempts to reach the surface, and attempts to get to shore without consideration of fatigue, cold, or buoyancy.

Usually panic develops gradually and is the end point of adaptive decay. This is not always true because a perfectly calm diver may panic due to a sudden air failure at 120 feet or due to the sighting of several great white sharks. A sudden, severe shock may cause a vagal response with a profound slowing of the heart. In some persons this slowing may actually stop the heart or cause abnormal rhythms. In the more typical case, the diver passes from fearfulness through severe anxiety to actual panic.

In panic, breathing becomes very rapid and shallow, like panting. This breathing does not actually ventilate the lungs and is, thus, different from hyperventilation with deep, rapid breathing. The breathing pattern in panic is ineffective and leads to a rise in carbon dioxide and a decrease in oxygen. Fatigue soon ensues.

After a possible early slowing, the heart rate increases because of central stimulation and because of the rising carbon dioxide. Disturbances in rhythm may result.

Muscular activity becomes frantic and ineffective, strength wanes. The activity deepens fatigue. Other basic physiologic responses include dilation of the pupils of the eyes, and rising levels of the stress hormones—steroids, adrenaline, and noradrenaline.

Once true panicked activity begins it becomes self-perpetuating. The rising carbon dioxide, falling oxygen, and fatigue drive the body to even more rapid breathing and frenzied muscular action.

A panicked diver cannot save himself. He will not use his emergency equipment. Unless promptly rescued he will drown or die of cardiac arrest.

Preventing Panic

Panic can be viewed as a maladapted response to stress. Prevention involves minimizing stress and improving response to it. Stress is usually an individual reaction. For example, a flooded mask means nothing to a good diver but could panic a novice. With experience, many of the challenges listed before fade from significance. One of the major goals in training should be to simply minimize things that frighten the diver. Anxiety begins in response to the perception of a dangerous situation. It does not matter whether the danger is real or imagined. The individual's "feelings" are what make the difference between calm and fearful diving.

Training does help the diver narrow his range of frightening experiences and teaches him how to react to stressful situations. The flooded mask is recognized as a minor problem that can be easily and quickly remedied. Training involves lectures, discussions, pool work, and open water dives. Adequate training requires more diving than can be provided in a basic scuba class. Graduates should be encouraged to spend their first few months diving under supervision in an advanced class or with a club. Independent diving may be so stressful at first as to cause accidents or fear sufficient to force the diver to leave the sport.

Perception of danger and response to it is determined by an interaction of *mental state* and *physical capability*. These are so intertwined that separation is possible only for discussion purposes. Ideally, the graduate believes that diving is enjoyable and safe. He recognizes that dangers exist, and that they call for respect, not terror. A person who gets scared just thinking about diving can be expected to have trouble in the water. Amazingly, people who are afraid of the water do set out to become divers. Some of them even become certified without learning that diving is fun.

The instructor carries a great deal of responsibility for his students' attitudes toward diving. Heroic sea stories and over-emphasis on danger do not build self confidence in most students. Obviously, this does not mean that risks should be ignored, but rather, these risks be brought into perspective. Teaching all the water skills but leaving the student frightened proves the class a failure. The instructor's personal example provides a much more effective witness than any number of lectures. The instructor who enjoys diving, and does so with grace and calmness, serves a worthwhile model for impressionable students.

Students should not be made to feel that anxiety is abnormal or a sign of weakness. As discussed, anxiety is reasonable, normal, and helpful when controlled. Students should feel free to discuss their anxieties about diving without threat of ridicule.

Since extreme anxiety and panic cause a return to instinctive behavior, good diving habits should be well taught. Hopefully, unthinking actions will then be the proper actions. Certain areas need particular emphasis, including proper ascents and the use of buoyancy vests to stay afloat. The true learning of proper habits takes time. There is no simple way to ensure that the lessons have been learned.

Through the years harassment drills have been popular in some scuba classes. The instructor performs these little assaults such as turning off air and pulling masks off the students. Simplistically, these drills test the students' reactions to stress and hopefully convince them they can survive mishap. Unfortunately, harass-ment has a few drawbacks: the drills are not always comparable to actual diving emergencies; divers may be inappropriately frightened; instructors may not have the training to use harassment effectively; and certain drills are dangerous.

Instructor organizations need to evaluate thoughtfully the advantages and disadvantages of harassment. The goal may be very worthy; but the methods are somewhat suspect.

Physical capability affects both perception and action. A physically comfortable diver is less likely to be fearful. When he can enter the surf and swim without fatigue, the ocean seems a pleasant place. But the cold, exhausted, and seasick diver finds even small problems frightening. Any physical disability draws attention away from the task of diving. Disabilities and fear act together to induce panic.

Similarly, the fit diver can better deal with real emergencies. He has the strength to make unexpected swims and endurance to stay afloat if he should be carried out to sea. Physical fitness enhances mental fitness.

In the early days of scuba, almost everyone began by ocean swimming and skin diving. These activities developed mental and physical competence. Now some diving instructors entice persons who can barely swim to take a basic scuba class. The class should include fitness drills, but it can not, in a number of weeks, make a fine swimmer out of a beginner. A return to an emphasis on water skills would reduce the incidence of inappropriate fears and other diving problems.

Treating Panic

Proper treatment of panic requires prevention first. Divers who are substandard emotionally or physically should not enter open water. This requires self evaluation and/or evaluation by an instructor, buddy, or dive supervisor. Too many accidents include retrospective statements like: "I didn't feel good," "I was having trouble with my gear," "I didn't like the look of the surf," and "I felt dog tired after carrying the tanks to the beach."

Be aware of warning signals in yourself and in your companions. This observance of warning signals carries on into the dive. If the dive seems to be going poorly, follow these steps:

a. Stop or slow down.

b. Take a few, slow, deep breaths.

c. Reevaluate the situation. If you are underwater and still feel uneasy, make an unhurried ascent.

d. Inflate your vest if you feel heavy. Do not hesitate to ditch your weights if necessary.

e. Signal your buddy.

f. Quit the dive, if the above do not help.

These same steps can be applied to the case of the fearful buddy or student. Offer vocal reassurance. Many times this will resolve the problem. If necessary, assist with flotation. The early recognition of excessive anxiety can prevent panic. This, naturally, requires alertness on the part of everyone. No stigma of failure should be assigned to a diver who decides to quit a dive. Everyone has bad days. It is far better to miss one dive than to become so scared that you give up diving, or have a serious accident.

There is no self treatment for true panic. By that time rational thought and activity are impossible. Your only hope rests with an alert, trained companion.

Panic kills quickly and must not be ignored. You must quickly reach the victim and keep him above water. Firm reassurance may break the cycle. Be very cautious in approaching a panicked diver. In his frenzy, he may drag you under.

Nobody knows how many accidents result from panic. It, and advanced stages of fearfulness, no doubt cause or contribute to many accidents and fatalities. In a way, though, the term "panic" has become a wastebasket diagnosis used to explain any puzzling accident. Panic, by itself, rarely kills. It leads to death by drowning, embolism, and other tragedies. Panic management requires prevention, quick rescue of the panicked victim, and then the treatment of associated maladies.

4

Using Equipment Safely

"To my way of thinking, one of the greatest beauties of goggling is the primitive simplicity of the equipment. With a pair of goggles and a spear—at the most, five dollars' worth—you are all set . . ."
Guy Gilpatric, The Compleat Goggler, 1938.

"Diving is an equipment intensive sport." From a diving training newsletter, 1977.

During the forty years between the writing of Gilpatric's statement and the current jargon, diving equipment has changed beyond imagination. Almost any piece of equipment is available and those who prefer simplicity are ridiculed as "substandard divers." It would be overly cynical to comment that most of the new diving equipment chiefly benefits those who manufacture and sell it.

Modern, reliable equipment can actually promote safe diving. There is no doubt that some of the new equipment makes diving easier and consequently more fun. Using some of the new equipment, without proper training, can be dangerous. This chapter discusses the basic principles of equipment safety with some specific references. It is not a complete guide to diving equipment—a subject that could fill an entire book.

THE BASICS

Clothing is not necessarily a requirement, but cold and abrasion cancel much of the charm of nude diving. Suffice it to say that many warm water divers prefer the freedom of not wearing a suit. A diving suit serves three purposes: heat maintenance, protection from abrasions, and a source of buoyancy. The subject of cold water is discussed in chapter 10. Abrasion protection is a valuable service provided by a diving suit—look at the "dings" on your suit and be glad they are not on your skin! Divers who do not use suits often wear t-shirts or sweat shirts to reduce shoulder strap wear and protect their skins.

To see effectively underwater, the diver needs a mask. Poor visioned divers can use masks with corrective lenses. Contact lenses work nicely under a mask if you aren't afraid of losing them. Selection of a mask is a personal choice, not dictated by safety considerations. Do not try to dive with goggles. Water pressure will cause a facial squeeze. (*See chapter 7 on barotrauma.*)

Fins are not essential for diving, but they are very handy. Pick ones that you can manage easily; overestimating your strength may give you leg cramps. Recent changes in fin design are worth a comment. In the 1950s and 1960s, only children and tourists used adjustable strap fins. A Navy physician was almost laughed out of a class in 1968 because of his vented, adjustable fins. Today many divers use these fins.

Skin divers need a snorkel and they are useful for surface swimming in scuba diving. The choice is personal but the current plastic shortage has made it difficult to find snorkels with ping-pong ball valves.

A functional knife should be available to cut entanglements. Don't let the knife become entangled in weeds. Scuba divers also need an accurate depth gauge and diving watch to help prevent decompression sickness and nitrogen narcosis. These tools also assist in monitoring air supply.

Air Supply

Air supply is comprised of the compressed air and the tank in which it fits. In the early days of scuba, divers used all sorts of gas tanks with their homemade rigs. These tanks were often not satisfactory for the storage of high pressure breathing-grade air. Air tanks must be strong enough to withstand gas pressure, and they must be clean. Strong tanks are available in either steel or aluminum. They should be hydrostatically tested every five years. But, it is not sufficient to ignore your tank except for the hydrostatic tests. A visual inspection of the tank's interior should be made each year to be certain there is no visible corrosion. Metals corrode and this weakens the tanks and can foul the air. Aluminum tanks corrode more slowly than steel ones.

If moisture enters a steel tank, oxides of iron form and consume both the steel and the oxygen in the tank's air. Moisture enters from poorly filtered air compressors and from tanks that are run out of air. Storing the tank with compressed air in it prevents accidental introduction of wet air.

One diver died from using a tank in which huge quantities of corrosion had reduced the oxygen concentration to between two and three percent. The normal oxygen concentration in air is twenty-one percent.

Modern air stations supply pure air for scuba divers. Errors in filling include using the wrong gas or using impure gas. Patronize only reputable air stations. Failure to fill tanks correctly has resulted in tank explosions and fatalities. Do not overfill tanks; the results will also be explosion. Poorly vented or overheated oil-cooled compressors can contaminate the air with carbon monoxide. Carbon monoxide reduces oxygen availability in the body and causes hypoxic damage. Carbon monoxide poisoning develops insidiously since the symptoms of low oxygen may not appear before the loss of consciousness.

Taking Enough Air Along

Nothing spoils a scuba dive faster than running out of air. The submersible pressure gauge, one of the truly major advances in equipment, should prevent this. The projected air supply duration can be calculated by knowing how much air is in the tank, the depth of the dive, and the air consumption rate. Errors in all of these parameters are common. Often a diver grabs a tank and goes diving without even checking the pressure. The tank might have been short filled, partially used, filled hot (pressure then falls as the air cools), or even not filled at all.

During a typical dive, depth changes frequently and randomly. Divers vary widely in their air consumption and consumption varies within a given dive. Only continuous monitoring can prevent errors in air supply duration. The pressure gauges, which mount on the regulator's first stage, are quite reliable. Naturally, they must be read periodically, not just carried.

Of course, safe dives can be made without pressure gauges. An experienced diver can more accurately predict air supply duration and note increased breathing resistance as tank pressure falls. The old "J" valve reserve system works well if positioned properly during the fill (down) and positioned properly during the dive (up). It should not be stuck shut or triggered unknowingly. The pressure gauge does not prevent a careless diver from running out of air, but pressure gauges are representative of advancements in diving equipment.

Breathing Mixes

Recreational divers should use only compressed air in standard open circuit scubas. Commercial diving and military diving use specialized equipment to eliminate bubble trails, extend bottom time, prevent nitrogen narcosis, and shorten decompression requirements.

Oxygen is very toxic when breathed under pressure. Oxygen dives must be very shallow. If used in an open circuit scuba, oxygen does not prolong gas supply duration, since the exhaled oxygen is exhausted. Rebreathing the exhaled gas, after removing its carbon dioxide, does make longer dives possible. But this requires use of rebreathing apparatus which is less safe than open circuit for recreational diving. A malfunction in carbon dioxide absorption can cause carbon dioxide poisoning.

Mixed gas diving is not suitable for recreational use. The gas mix must be calculated for dive depth to prevent excessive or inadequate oxygen concentrations. Again, carbon dioxide absorption is used to conserve the expensive gas supply. For short, shallow dives, helium breathing requires more decompression than breathing nitrogen.

Regulators

There are many different regulators currently on the market and new ones are introduced continually. All have features that would turn early scuba divers green with envy. Any available regulators will do an adequate job. However, strenuous deeper dives exceed the potential of some regulators. Impartial testing would help, but it is just starting to be done. Most divers are using single hose regulators in preference to the two hose regulators. Really, the only advantage of a two hose regulator is that you never get bubbles in your field of vision. It is more difficult to use a submersible pressure gauge with a two hose regulator.

Divers should use a standard regulator and not try to modify it. Regulators should be kept in proper working order at all times. Fatal accidents have been attributed to non-standard, poorly maintained regulators.

Octopus regulators, with a second regulator attached to the first stage of the primary regulator, are discussed in chapter 6.

FLOTATION AND BUOYANCY CONTROL

The equipment used for flotation and buoyancy control has probably undergone the most improvement in the short history of scuba diving. Equipment has been modified, and basic safety concepts have been challenged. Challenge usually brings positive change. The gogglers of Gilpatric's era didn't worry about artificial flotation devices. With time, the idea developed that skin divers needed a safety vest that could be inflated in an emergency. Small vests were introduced that could be inflated by mouth or with a small carbon dioxide cylinder. These vests were intended for surface use. Their size and the size of the inflating cylinder made them ineffective as a means of making buoyant, emergency ascents. Thousands of divers learned that the safety vest was put on first over the suit so that if everything else had to be ditched, the vest was still available for use. Most of these divers found that their carbon dioxide inflators corroded quickly and rarely worked unless very carefully maintained. A few divers found they could orally inflate their vests on the surface and make it easier to stay afloat. This may have started the movement to view the vest as a tool rather than a piece of emergency equipment.

In time, the term "safety vest" became declassé and "buoyancy compensator" entered the diver's vocabulary. A buoyancy compensator is an inflatable device, originally a vest design, that can be used to adjust the "trim" during a dive. Buoyancy, of course, is the floating force exerted on an object by the sea that depends on the volume of water displaced by the object. Blowing up a vest increases displacement and increases upward force. This offsets loss of buoyancy through suit compression or by increased weight from picking up things from the ocean bottom. The vest can be inflated orally, by a low pressure line from the regulator's first stage, or by a separate vest inflating tank. The buoyancy compensator can be used underwater and on the surface. Compensators have been modified to include back mounted devices and wrap arounds that combine vest and back mounted features.

Although not designed as emergency devices, these compensators generally provide enough lift to give a rapid trip to the surface. Orally inflated compensators are not very efficient for emergency ascents, and compensators that fill from the regulator do not work when the tank air supply is depleted. Buoyant ascents are the most dangerous form of emergency ascent. They are discussed in chapter 9.

The era of buoyancy compensators seems to be upon us. They can definitely make diving easier, but they are not without problems. Inexperienced divers often get confused between inflating and deflating and go in the wrong direction. Any piece of equipment can malfunction. A tank inflated compensator is useless in skin diving, especially if it doesn't have a carbon dioxide cylinder for emergency flotation. Some proponents of the back mounted devices suggest that they can be ditched in an emergency. This, of course, leaves the diver without any flotation device.

The biggest drawback of some compensators is that they may float an incapacitated diver face down in the water. This is especially likely with the back mounted compensators. Amazingly, the designers of these compensators don't view this as a hazard. It is not good for an unconscious diver to be floated face down in the water. A buoyancy compensator may be a tool, but it shouldn't be a weapon in an emergency.

About half of the diving fatalities, according to statistics, are found with non-inflated vests. This suggests that either the diver did not think to inflate the vest, he was physically or mentally incapacitated, or the vest malfunctioned. Some of the vests, indeed, proved to be defective, but this was only a small portion of the total number. In physical incapacitation such as a stroke or an embolism, the diver might suddenly be unconscious. Only an alert buddy could inflate his flotation device and this requires a familiarity with the device. A good diving buddy should be observant of his buddy's condition and know the other's gear.

Most disasters start gradually and during the early phases, the diver should inflate the flotation device. The high failure rate implies the diver did not recognize the need for flotation or that he was too upset to work the vest. Even in an early panic state, some divers stop thinking well. Unless the need to inflate is basic in his mind, he won't do it. And, if the task is at all complex, he won't be capable of completing it. Diving classes must thoroughly teach the use of flotation equipment. This is a difficult task because of the variety available. A diver who buys or rents an unfamiliar compensator should practice with it before going into open water.

Diving suits provide quite a bit of buoyancy on the surface. Suits compress with descent and buoyancy decreases.* The suit

---

*A skin diver's chest compresses with descent further decreasing buoyancy. This is the old "bottom drop." Scuba divers do not have chest compression because they breathe regularly.

decreases by fifty percent in the first thirty-three feet. Thus a diver who is neutrally buoyant on the surface will be heavy at depth. This makes descent easy and ascent more difficult. Normally, a little kicking will offset the heaviness. A buoyancy compensator can be used to offset the loss of suit volume.

Weight Systems

Divers wear weights to counteract the buoyant force of the ocean and their suits. Because of differences in body build, persons vary in their weight requirements when using the same equipment. Lean, muscular divers have less natural buoyancy than short, obese divers.

The diver usually chooses to be neutral at the surface. He can float without effort. Taking a breath increases his buoyancy and causes him to rise in the water. Exhaling causes him to sink slightly. At depth the neutral surface buoyancy becomes negative buoyancy. Going light on the surface, by using less weight, makes descent harder but makes ascent easy. Weighing heavy on the surface is not advisable as it intensifies the natural heaviness at depth.

Divers have been taught to put the weight belt on last and to ditch it in an emergency. Unfortunately in most fatalities studied, the victim has failed to drop the belt. This results from several other problems including:

a. Sudden physical injury rendered the diver helpless.

b. The belt became twisted or entangled and would not drop free.

c. The diver was using weights in canisters that do not drop free.

The diver knows weights should be ditched in emergencies but in panic states this rational thinking stops. At an earlier moment he might have made the decision to drop the weights, but didn't recognize that things were getting worse. Suddenly, physical injury may make dumping even a functional belt impossible. Very often, releasing the belt buckle doesn't result in the belt dropping free. There are a myriad of reasons for this. The belt goes on last and must not be impinged by any other gear. Practice dropping the belt, on land, while wearing all your equipment. Better still, practice this in the water after your equipment has shifted about. Cloth belts usually rotate and the buckle is not quickly available. The old "cheapo" diver still has a primitive vest, but he loves his new rubber belt because it stays in place during every dive.

Because divers often fail to ditch weights, some instructors have suggested stopping the emphasis on it during training. The logic is obviously defective. Students need to learn how to wear their weights correctly and know how to get rid of them. They *must* be convinced that belts are expendable and should be ditched in the early stages of distress. Some divers are afraid to drop their weights while underwater because they will "rocket to the surface." The fallacy in this thinking should be demonstrated in class. The ditching of weights will definitely speed ascent, especially near the surface, but it is easily controlled.

Some of the new, fancy compensators have weights as an integral part of the unit. They can only be dumped when in the vertical position—head up—and have been known to stick. The manufacturer may not view this as a problem, but prudent divers realize it is a serious design deficiency.

The buddy must be prepared to release his partner's weights. This requires familiarity with his weight system.

5

First Aid for Divers

A glance through the doctor's log on a trip in the Bahamas gives an idea of the first aid problems commonly encountered in diving. The week was marred by two cut fingers from boat handling mishaps, a bumped head from a swinging boom, six cases of severe sunburn, and a few headaches.

Quick action by onlookers prevented the drowning of a tourist who thought he didn't need to know how to swim in order to dive! No one had decompression sickness, air embolism, carbon monoxide poisoning, or thoracic squeeze.

Divers have a special need for first aid skills. They are frequently far away from medical care and in an unfamiliar environment. Divers need to know how to treat minor ailments and how to maintain victims of major accidents until help can be obtained. Standard first aid courses prepare divers to handle most emergencies, which should be adequate for all but a few accidents. Reading is no substitute for practice. Classes provide an opportunity to practice skills until they become familiar.

Each diving party should travel with a first aid kit. The kit should be placed on the beach or in the boat in a spot convenient to all divers. The list of specific items to include will vary depending on the nature and location of the dive. Some items include:

- a blanket
- small adhesive bandages
- sterile gauze pads and triangular bandages
- adhesive tape
- scissors, tweezers, and thermometer
- air splint for arms and legs
- rubbing alcohol, germicidal soap, and a small brush

33

For dives in really remote areas an oxygen cylinder with a mask and auto-inflating bag (or manual respirator valve) should also be included. Expedition dives obviously receive more equipment.

Each diver should have a basic competence in first aid. Accidents can occur before, during, and after the dive—it is best to be prepared for any and all accidents that could happen.

Sunburn

Staying indoors prevents sunburn, but it is neither fun nor practical for divers. Divers must learn to deal safely with the elements. Around open water, burning is especially a problem because of surface reflection. Cloudy days do not screen the burning ultraviolet rays; wind makes the skin cool, but increases the likelihood of sunburn. Chronic exposure to sun damages the skin cells and may start skin cancer even without burning. But most people want suntans and there *are* ways to do it safely. Graduated exposure time is best. Tropical sun burns quickly and sun time should be limited to a few minutes the first day. Burning becomes evident only after exposure, so do not wait until it hurts before covering up.

Many chemical sunscreens offer some protection. Opaque types, such as zinc oxide, protect well but are not practical for total body coverage. The more popular suntan products do not work well for divers because they wash off once the diver enters the water. The newer para-aminobenzoic acid (PABA) products have been a major improvement. They stay on the skin better and do a much more complete job of blocking ultraviolet rays, but these products will not protect completely so caution is necessary. After prolonged diving they should be reapplied. Some will stain clothes, but not wet suits. Unfortunately some people have contact dermatitis from PABA products and some users suffer burning and itching after sun exposure. Test any new product for several days before the dive and talk to your doctor if you have had skin disorders.

When sunburn does occur it should be treated carefully. Do not worsen it by going back into the sun. Most physicians advise against applications of "burn" ointments or other chemicals; but a cold compress will relieve the pain. If blisters develop, it is best not to open them as they easily become infected. Severe sunburn may cause symptoms such as fever, nausea, and vomiting. Such severe cases may require medical attention. Severe sunburn is not a trivial problem, and should not be treated as such.

Seasickness

Some "fair weather" divers think that seasickness only occurs during boat trips to and from diving sites. One dive in the rolling coastal seas would convince them that seasickness can present problems while diving. Symptoms of seasickness fall into two inter-related groups, and divers can exhibit symptoms for either or both groups. They include physical symptoms and behavioral symptoms.

Physical susceptibility varies widely, but all persons with normal vestibular systems can become seasick. Seasickness typically begins with skin paleness and then progresses to cold sweating, nausea, and finally vomiting. Divers often fail to recognize any symptom until nausea and vomiting, though careful recall often reveals previous symptoms. Behavioral consequences of seasickness include: listlessness, unclear thinking, and low morale. Victims with the same physical disability may vary widely in their ability to continue normal activities through the duration of the illness.

Seasickness is caused by stimulation of the vestibular apparatus of the ear. Many people seem to have motion effects intensified by other factors including posture, engine fumes, and the sight of others being sick.

With continued stimulation the body becomes adapted to motion and the incidence of seasickness decreases. Thus, the first few days of an ocean trip are usually the hardest. Unfortunately, this adaptation is quickly lost. Making a dive one week does not keep the diver in shape for dive a week later.

There are, however, several things a diver can do to try to prevent seasickness.

Avoid diving on days when the sea is rough. Avoidance, obviously, is often the best preventive medicine—but it is not always fun.

Take seasickness prevention medicine. Several drugs offer some protection against the malady, but again, individual response to these drugs varies widely. *Never* use a drug for diving without having land-tested its effects first. Unfortunately, you may find that many seasickness medications are unsuitable for diving because they induce drowsiness.

Maintain proper diet controls. Despite some scientific disclaimers that diet is not linked with seasickness, most divers find that it is. Large, fatty meals appear to cause more distress than light, bland meals. Starvation diets, however, have not been effective in preventing the illness, because divers need food energy.

Once a diver becomes ill, however, there is little to do but end the dive immediately.

External Ear Infections

Repeated water immersion can lead to infections of the ear canal. Water removes the protective cerumen and macerates the tissues. This results in a change in the canal's bacterial population and aids in the development of external otitis or "swimmer's ear."

Infections develop even in clean water and are usually bacterial though fungi may be a problem in warm, humid climates. Most divers avoid infection because they do not spend that much time in the water, but the incidence approaches 100 percent in saturation divers.

Prevention can be simple. Do not use swabs to dry or clean your ears. These swabs remove cerumen and damage the canal lining. The ear normally cleans itself. Many divers use ear drops to dry and acidify the ears after a dive. These drops usually consist of acetic acid in alcohol (or propylene glycol) or aluminum and calcium acetate. No one has proved the effectiveness of these drops.

External ear infections usually become noticeable by pain in the ear which is intensified by moving the ear lobe. Examination may reveal scaling and discharge. Ear pain after a diving trip should be evaluated by a physician so that the possibility of ear injuries can be caught and treated early. External ear infections are treated by drying the canal and applying antibiotic drops (often combined with steroids). Healing proceeds more effectively if the diver stays away from water until the infection has completely cleared. Divers should not use ear plugs to protect the ear canals. This is discussed in detail in chapter 7.

PRINCIPLES OF ACCIDENT MANAGEMENT

By their nature, accidents occur at the wrong place, at the wrong time. You may dive for years without seeing anything more serious than a scraped toe, then see two fatalities in a matter of weeks. When you come upon your first accident, you may feel frightened and uncertain of your first aid skills. A few basic principles should be remembered in dealing with accidents.

Be prepared and willing to help. Keep your skills current. Each diver should know the location of the nearest emergency medical facility, and the nearest decompression chamber. First aid kits should be standard equipment on all diving trips.

Avoid making the situation worse. Be careful about moving people who have been thrown against rocks or slammed into the sand by a wave. In your eagerness to get the victim in a better position to dress a hand wound, you may aggravate a spinal fracture.

Establish priorities of treatment. Certain medical problems require more prompt action than others. When you come upon an accident, spend a few moments to evaluate the situation. The most obvious problem (such as a cut wrist) may be less important than a more obscure one (the victim is not breathing). Don't spend a lot of time making a diagnosis—just take a good look around and take care of the most serious problem first. If the victim is not breathing, your first step is to begin resuscitation; worry about the cut wrist later.

Remember basic concepts before minute details. A helpful way to remember the organization of emergency care is to remember the *ABCs,* (airway, breathing, and circulation). The victim needs an open airway for air entry. In unconsciousness or convulsions, the airway may be mechanically blocked (usually by the tongue, but sometimes by a foreign object) even through the chest moves spontaneously. Tilting the head back and moving the lower jaw forward may make the victim's own breathing efforts effective. *Be very careful* about moving the head and neck, especially if there is the possibility of a neck fracture. Opening the airway has precedence, but be very cautious about doing it. If position does not open the airway, reach into the mouth and remove any obstructing objects.

All this should take only seconds since a prompt decision must be made regarding the need for artificial ventilation. When the victim is not breathing or taking very shallow breaths, mouth-to-mouth or mouth-to-nose ventilation should be started immediately. (Techniques will be discussed in chapter 6.) *Seconds count;* do not waste time waiting for equipment or assistance. When the airway has been opened and ventilation begun, check the action of the heart. As you ventilate feel for a pulse or have someone else do it. This is difficult to do with gloves on especially when the victim is wearing a hooded wet suit. When necessary, begin cardiac compression. Cardiac massage is more serious than artificial ventilation. However, if you are unsure of the victim's pulse, and he turns blue despite effective ventilation, compression *must* be done.

Only after the ABCs are established should attention be turned to other problems. Bleeding should be controlled. There is little need to worry about bleeding initially, since it will stop soon after ventilation ceases and the patient has no blood pressure. Active bleeding is good news because it indicates a functioning circulatory system.

Often the exact nature of the accident will be unclear at the onset. This presents few problems for the organized rescuer who goes to work on the symptoms and signs instead of wringing his hands in dismay that the victim doesn't look like anything in the first aid class. Victims often have several different types of injuries; for example, the nearly drowned diver with an air embolism. Support life first and then try for a diagnosis.

Get professional help for serious problems. In minor accidents first aid may solve the problem, but professional help should be consulted for more serious problems. Initial care can often relieve pain—but a follow up appointment with a professional should be arranged to assure that there are no complications or undetected problems. If there is the slightest doubt about the treatment, consult a physician at the first possible moment.

Be certain that your efforts don't complicate further care. An incorrectly applied tourniquet may cause vessel or nerve damage. Improper cardiac compression may lacerate the liver. *Do not give victims alcohol.* It does not warm them, just the opposite. Alcohol depresses the mental state, makes evaluation difficult, and may obscure injuries. Accident victims in fact, should not be given any food or drink. If emergency surgery is necessary this ingestion complicates anesthesia by making pulmonary aspiration likely. Even liquids may not be absorbed. Giving fluids does not help and it can often create very serious problems.

It will help the emergency physician if notes are taken at the accident site regarding the nature of the dive, what happened, how the victim appeared, what was done, and how the victim responded. Writing information down takes only a few minutes and provides a better record than relying on memory and greatly assists in diagnosis and treatment.

POSITIONING AND GENERAL CARE

Verify breathing and pulse then perform cardiopulmonary resuscitation, if required. If the victim is in a hazardous area, gently move him away from the area. If there are possible neck or spine injuries, leave the victim on his back and do not permit movement of the spine. In other cases, a position on the left side is good since it provides a better airway, protects against aspiration of vomiting during sickness. Putting the feet up and the trunk and head down provides protection against aspiration. It also increases circulatory volume by shifting blood away from the legs. It may provide some protection against embolization of the brain though most bubbles probably have lodged before the position is assumed. But this tilt position makes breathing somewhat more difficult since abdominal contents are shifted against the diaphragm. Upper body bleeding may also increase in the tilt position. This is especially true of head injuries.

Loosen clothing, especially the wet suit, so that the victim can breathe freely and you can easily observe breathing patterns and pulse.

Exposure of a wet person on a cold beach quickly causes severe chilling. Blankets or towels should be provided to reduce heat loss. Do not offer liquids unless the injury is trivial. Do not treat someone and then stop paying attention to them. Watch them carefully for breathing, pulse, consciousness, vomiting, renewed bleeding, or seizures. Conscious victims need reassurance and guidance, assure them they will be taken care of.

Once the emergency has stabilized, you need to consider transportation for follow-up care. If there are other divers in your group, this can be accomplished while you are busy. If you dive in a populated area, it is generally better to permit an ambulance or paramedic unit to transport the victim. Do not abandon the patient. Remember that what you know about the accident can be very important to the victim's physician.

Generally the best first destination is a hospital rather than a recompression chamber. Hospitals are, of course, more common and they provide facilities for careful examination and evaluation. Only rarely is immediate recompression necessary. This does not excuse undue delay in obtaining the necessary hyperbaric therapy. Diving in remote areas can cause even more serious problems in accident management.

Expedition diving requires that all participants be well versed in first aid techniques and adequate equipment (especially oxygen) be immediately available for lengthy transportation. It is essential to know the location and availability of reliable medical facilities and how to arrange for prompt transportation to them. Time becomes much more an issue when dealing with accidents in remote areas.

Specific Emergencies

Unconsciousness. The unconscious diver provides a frightening and complex challenge to the first aider. Initially disregard the cause of unconsciousness and institute the general principles discussed earlier. Once you have stabilized the victim, attention can be directed to the accident's cause. There are a myriad of reasons for unconsciousness and no one remembers all of them. Some of the more common reasons include head injury, non-diving maladies (such as stroke, heart attack, hypoglycemia, or epilepsy) hypoxia from drowning, hypoxia from poor air supply, hyperventilation, or heart arrhythmia, air embolism, and decompression sickness.

All causes except air embolism and decompression sickness require first aid and then standard intensive hospital care. The unconscious scuba diver is initially managed in the same way, but then needs recompression. Unless proven otherwise, the unconscious scuba diver usually has air embolism or decompression sickness. Air embolism is more likely than decompression sickness to result in unconsciousness.

The initial recompression management of these accidents is the same, but if possible a differentiation should be made since the decompression phases differ markedly. A skilled hyperbaric therapist may be able to make the diagnosis on physical findings, but a good history of the dive is most helpful.

Answers to the following questions may provide needed information to make the differentiation.

● *How deep was the dive?* Embolism is possible from any depth. Decompression sickness is unlikely in less than thirty-three feet of water.

● *How long was the dive?* Decompression sickness requires a certain depth and time combination. Embolism has no time requirement.

● *Was the diver in distress underwater?* A positive answer makes embolism likely since a diver in trouble can easily make an improper ascent. Of course, a diver who needed decompression stops might have missed them due to the need for a rapid ascent.

● *Was the diver making an emergency ascent (either real or simulated)?* The incidence of embolism increases markedly during emergency ascents.

One of the buddy's roles is knowing what his partner is doing underwater. The therapist knows that impressions sometimes become hazy after the accident and that dive depth and time measurements are notoriously inaccurate.

Prompt recompression to 165 feet will quickly restore consciousness to the embolism victim and relieve any signs of damage. Response may be slower in decompression sickness. But if treatment is delayed, response may be prolonged in air embolism victims; hence, response time is not too reliable a guide.

Be sure the emergency room physicians know the patient was scuba diving. There have been tragic delays in obtaining definitive treatment because the possibility of air embolism or decompression sickness have not been considered.

Central Nervous System Injury

Central nervous system (brain and spinal cord) injuries often occur without unconsciousness. Findings include altered mental state, dizziness, convulsions, poor coordination, hearing impairment, and weakness or paralysis. Any central nervous injury is significant. They may come from trauma, non-diving maladies, hypoxia, air embolism, or decompression sickness.

A word should be said about the nervous, frightened diver who complains of shortness of breath, generalized weakness, and tingling fingers. This may well be a case of hyperventilation in which the carbon dioxide levels fall drastically. If the diver can be calmed and begins to breathe normally, the symptoms quickly resolve.

A diver with convulsions needs protection so the seizures do not result in cuts or fractures. Repeated seizures may cause airway and ventilation problems. Dizziness and hearing impairment may be signs of ear barotrauma or central nervous system decompression sickness. In any event medical evaluation should be prompt.

Drowning leads to hypoxia and this may cause any of the central nervous system findings. The scuba diver with any central nervous system impairment needs recompression. Cases of air embolism that had only minor reflex abnormality have been reported. Both embolism and decompression can be progressive and a minor symptom may be just a warning of worse to come. Do not delay treatment.

Head and Neck Injuries

These injuries usually occur during water entry or exit. Divers crack their heads on boat hulls, against rocks, or get their heads jammed into the sand by the surf. Often the first evidence of injury will be an obvious cut or scrape. But, unconsciousness may also be the first sign.

There is no way to overemphasize the importance of injuries to the vertebral column (neck and spine). The vertebrae protect the spinal cord and bone injuries often damage the spinal cord. These spinal cord injuries usually do not heal. Any violent trauma can cause spinal injuries. A great many of them follow mishaps in the surf.

A spinal cord injury causes paralysis (sometimes just weakness) and sensory impairment below the injury. If you give first aid to a person complaining of weakness or numbness, be alert to the likelihood of spinal injury. The neck can be broken without any cord damage. However, improper movement may then destroy the spinal cord. *Be very gentle in moving any trauma victim.* Do not permit the head and the neck to move about. When performing cardiopulmonary resuscitation, consider the possibility of neck injury before tilting the head.

Head injuries tend to be progressive, so continued observation of any possible head injury is essential. The development of bleeding from the ears is strongly suggestive of a skull fracture. This bleeding would be more copious and persistent than with a ruptured ear drum. Mental states may deteriorate and the pupils of the eyes become uneven in size. Vomiting and aspiration are major hazards in head injuries.

Bleeding and Wound Care

Most bleeding accidents in diving are not life threatening with the exception of propeller injuries or spear gun wounds. Bleeding occurs from either veins or arteries. Arterial bleeding becomes serious much more quickly and is more difficult to control because of the higher pressure in arteries. Arterial blood squirts rather than flows and is brighter red in color. Serious bleeding may be unobserved in fractures and in the gastrointestinal tract.

Even minor bleeding will be disastrous if it is not controlled. After significant blood loss, the skin becomes pale, cool, and dry. The pulse feels weak and is usually rapid. The brain is protected, but eventually it, too, shows the results of inadequate blood volume.

Most bleeding can be controlled by direct pressure over the wound. Use a gauze pad or a clean cloth. What about pressure points? People usually forget where pressure points are and find it difficult to utilize them. Pressure must be maintained until the bleeding stops. All but large or deep cuts seal themselves, but this takes time. Do not keep releasing wound pressure to see if the bleeding has stopped because this disturbs clotting and prolongs the bleeding. A pressure dressing can be tied over the wound, but care must be taken to get it tight enough. Too much pressure, however, can damage surrounding tissues.

Elevating extremity wounds above heart level reduces the driving force for bleeding. Very severe bleeding may require a tourniquet for control. Tourniquets are dangerous since they compress nerves and may damage extremities by obstructing their blood supply. Tourniquets, used when other methods do not stop the bleeding, can be life saving. Do not watch someone bleed to death because you are afraid of applying a tourniquet. Extremities can tolerate more than an hour of ischemia and this should provide time to reach a facility where the bleeding can be professionally treated. These rules should be followed:

a. Use a tourniquet only if direct pressure fails.
b. Use a wide band, not a piece of string, to minimize damage to the underlying structures.
c. Make the tourniquet tight enough to block arterial flow. Otherwise blood will enter the limb and be forced out the wound.
d. Do not cover up tourniquets or forget you placed one.
e. Do not release the tourniquet every few minutes. An injury requiring one does not seal quickly. The frequent releasing just destroys any natural healing. Leave it thirty minutes initially and then loosen it to check for cessation of bleeding. Retighten if necessary.

Wounds should be kept clean, but do not restart bleeding by vigorous scrubbing. A germicidal soap is better than an antibiotic ointment for first aid. All but minor wounds should be seen by a physician because tetanus shots may be needed. If the wound requires stitches it should be done early to minimize the risk of infection—some dirty wounds are deliberately not stitched. Coral injuries heal poorly. Remove every bit of coral or the wound will fester.

Fractures

Broken bones can result from injuries during the actual dive, as well as entries or exits. During a recent diving rescue workshop, one participant broke his ankle by stepping into a small hole in shallow water.

Usually a fracture is obvious because of its sudden occurrence and the pain, deformity, and impaired motion associated with it. When in doubt, always treat as though a fracture is present. No harm is done by giving fracture first aid to a sprain.

First aid requires immobilization of the fracture and nonuse of the injured limb. Failure to observe these two principles may result in pain, worsening of the fracture, and damage to muscles, nerves, or blood vessels. Splinting the area and joints above and below the fracture is the best way to immobilize it. Virtually any rigid article can be used as a splint. Air splints are nice because they can be easily transported and are simple to apply.

Professional care is obviously necessary for any fracture, but time is especially important when dealing with several more severe fractures. Fractures of the spine, pelvis, thigh (femur), and joints are to be dealt with as soon as possible. Open compound fractures are also important and should be dealt with immediately. These open wounds should be kept clean at all times.

Injuries from Animals

Animals can cause harm to divers, but the number of harmful animals in U.S. waters is relatively small. Divers who explore foreign waters should learn about the animal life before they go abroad.

Biting injuries most commonly come from sharks, eels, and octopi. Shark bites cause potentially fatal injuries. Treatment involves control of bleeding and prevention of infection. Prudent divers stay away from sharks.

Unlike sharks, eels are not aggressive. They will protect their homes and they do not like hands stuck in their faces. An eel bite causes pain and severe bleeding. Like the eel, the octopus is not aggressive. They will bite if bothered but usually this is not a major problem, except with the poisonous Australian octopus.

The most commonly encountered stinging animal is the jellyfish. These primitive animals have venom contained in nematocysts which "fire" upon contact. Even a dead jellyfish can sting. Nematocysts may get on the outside of a wet suit and become apparent only when the diver undresses. Usually the stings are just painful but severe poisoning can be fatal.

Stay away from jellyfish if you see them. Treatment from a

sting involves removing any accumulated tentacles. Alcohol in-
activates the nematocysts so that they can be removed painlessly.
Do not rub the skin with sand as this makes the nematocysts fire.
Meat tenderizer has been used as a home cure. If symptoms
progress beyond localized pain and tenderness do not delay seek-
ing medical assistance.

Stingray injuries are common in beach divers who enter the
water without booties. The ray spine causes a painful wound
which is prone to infection. Occasionally systemic symptoms
develop and death has resulted. The wound must be cleansed
very well. Stingray toxin is destroyed by heat and soaking the injured foot in hot (but not too hot) water, will ease the pain.
Soak foot for 30 minutes. This usually brings relief.

In Hawaii and points west, poisonous cone shells threaten the
careless collector. Since their bite can be very serious, handle all
cones with heavy gloves and grab the broad end of the shell.

In warm waters scorpionfish, stonefish and lionfish, can cause
poisonous injury from venom in their spines. Extreme pain progresses to respiratory distress. Divers visiting tropical waters should
know what these fish look like and steer clear of fish that seem
fearless.

Regardless of the diving site, divers should be familiar with the
animal life on the surrounding beaches and in the waters.

6

Rescues and Resuscitations

In simplest terms drowning results from man's inability to obtain oxygen from water. If, for any reason, the skin or scuba diver runs out of air, drowning is likely. Drowning is defined as death by suffocation in a fluid, usually water. By convention, the term near-drowning describes a potential drowning reversed before death. Near-drowning can progress to actual drowning.

The first steps in drowning depend on the circumstances of the accident. If an alert person gets a mouth full of water, he struggles to get his head back above water. Reflexes cause his vocal cords to shut tightly and this keeps water out of the trachea, bronchi, and lungs. He holds his breath. If the episode is brief, such as being tumbled in the surf, the damage amounts to only some swallowed water.

Naturally, no one has actually studied human drowning in the laboratory so observations must be transferred from animal experiments. If submersion continues past the initial breath holding, the animals become desperate for air and may resume gasping breathing efforts. Reflexes still protect the lungs. Within a short time, however, hypoxia (low tissue oxygen levels) develop and the reflexes fail. Water enters into the lungs, and interrupts gas exchange. Without a continuous oxygen supply, heart action quickly stops and death soon follows.

Persons who become unconscious underwater may continue to breathe and will not struggle. Reflexes, however, still close the vocal cords unless the state of unconsciousness is very deep. Again hypoxia eventually blocks the reflexes and water enters into the lungs.

Unfortunately, a great deal of confusion exists about the importance of the reflex vocal cord closure. The process is called laryngospasm and is a normal, protective response to stimulation of the vocal cords. The term is misleading since the larynx (sometimes called the voice box) does not go into spasm. It is the vocal cords at the top of the larynx that spasm. Laryngospasm is an ambivalent reflex. It protects the lower air passages but it also causes damage by preventing air entry.

Can divers die in laryngospasm without getting water into their lungs? Some people think so and this may account for up to ten percent of drownings (so called "dry drownings"). Animal experiments, however, do not support this theory—drowned and nearly drowned animals showed water aspirated into their lungs. Clinical observations of anesthetized humans reveals that laryngospasm will consistently relax before respiratory or cardiac failure. Of course, this opening of the vocal cords doesn't help the submerged victim.

Even small amounts of water in the lungs cause severe defects in oxygenation of the blood. About 150 milliliters of water (five ounces) in an average person's lungs causes lowered blood oxygen. More than eighty-five percent of drowned persons apparently have only 1,500 milliliters or less of water in their lungs. The resultant hypoxia gradually disrupts functioning of all the body's systems. Water damages the lungs so that even prompt retrieval and resuscitation may not be effective. In one large group in the 1960s, twenty-five of those who were initially resuscitated eventually died. Modern therapy has greatly increased the chances of survival if resuscitation is prompt.

Formerly, a great deal of concern centered on whether the near-drowning took place in salt or fresh water. This difference turned out to be of little significance in treatment. Interestingly, it takes only half as much salt as fresh water to drown a dog.

DROWNING

Any mishap which interferes with air supply in the water can lead to drowning. Skin divers drown when they run out of air and cannot come back to the surface. Scuba divers drown if they stop using their scuba. Scuba deaths may be due to equipment failure or personal malfunction. Both scuba and skin divers also drown during water entries and exits and on swims to and from the dive site. It would be virtually impossible to list all the causes of drowning. The following list notes some of the more common causes.

Causes of surface drowning include:

a. surf injury in sand or rocks leading to incapacitation
b. being carried away by a current so far that return is impossible
c. exhaustion
d. panic
e. severe muscle cramps
f. animal injuries
g. intoxication or drug effects
h. heart attack, stroke, epilepsy, or other medical disorder
i. unconsciousness after air embolism
j. catastrophic decompression sickness (unusual in sport diving)

Underwater drownings can be caused by:

a. unconsciousness
b. panic
c. entanglement
d. equipment malfunction
e. being trapped out of air in a cave, wreck, or under ice

Drownings may also be classified by the state of "consciousness" before drowning. Conscious near-drowning victims most commonly are in one of these groups: exhausted, entangled, or panicked.

Obviously, a person could be in all three states at once. If for any reason such as fatigue, conditions of the sea, illness, or cold, a diver becomes exhausted, he may easily drown. These accidents generally occur on the surface and include the large number of swimmers who "just stop swimming and sink." With profound exhaustion the diver stops acting rationally. He forgets, or thinks he can't make the effort. He forgets that ditching the weight belt will enable his wet suit to keep him afloat. He may not inflate his vest if he is wearing one.

Entanglement can occur on the surface, but it is much more likely to be a problem underwater. Divers become entangled in any number of ways, but most commonly they are caught in kelp, weeds, or lines. The cave, wreck, or ice diver who cannot find his route to the surface should be considered an entangled diver. It is difficult to imagine a more terrifying way to end a diving career. Fully alert, but helpless.

Almost everyone has had a brief tangle in the kelp and knows the momentary fright associated with it. The trapped diver soon loses calmness and struggles wildly. This panicked behavior leads to exhaustion and increases air consumption. Of course, the skin diver is especially unable to tolerate prolonged entanglement. But even scuba divers with their external air supply are not immune. Ten percent of scuba deaths have some component of entanglement. This rises to twenty percent if cave divers are included.

Panic usually contributes to the drownings of the conscious divers and can be the start of virtually all diving maladies. For more complete treatment, see chapter 3 on panic.

Unconscious Divers

Divers may be unconscious before they start drowning. There are numerous causes for unconsciousness including trauma, illness, low oxygen intake, hyperventilation, or high carbon dioxide intake. Carbon monoxide poisoning, abnormal heart activity, air embolism, and decompression sickness can also be factors leading to unconsciousness during a dive.

Divers are subject to injuries and illnesses not directly related to diving. Head injuries from running into rocks, the bottom, or a boat hull can cause unconsciousness. Medical injuries include heart attack, strokes, epilepsy, low blood sugar, and drug reactions. Careful medical screening eliminates the obvious unfit from diving, but anyone can have a normal medical history and pass a physical and still suffer from the maladies just listed.

Complete prevention of medical unconsciousness is impossible but the risk can be decreased through medical examination and by convincing divers not to dive when they feel ill.

Skin divers will try anything to increase dive time. A common effective technique is hyperventilating before breath holding. This lowers the body's carbon dioxide which prolongs the time until carbon dioxide reaches the point where the urge to breathe becomes uncontrollable. Hyperventilation does not appreciably increase oxygen levels.

During a skin dive, blood oxygen steadily falls while carbon dioxide rises. After hyperventilation the delayed restoration of carbon dioxide may permit oxygen to fall to levels causing unconsciousness. Very low oxygen stimulates breathing, but consciousness may be lost before this point. After unconsciousness carbon dioxide still rises and the diver will eventually start to breathe. Unfortunately, he will inhale water. This process has caused many accidents in underwater swimming contests.

In diving, another phenomenon increases the risk. During a breathhold dive, lung compression raises the lung oxygen pressure. This pressure is responsible for transfer of oxygen to the blood. Thus a diver may be fine on the bottom, but suffer a severe reduction in oxygen on ascent with resulting unconsciousness. Unconsciousness from a breathholding hyperventilation is simple to prevent. Avoid vigorous hyperventilation. Do not hyperventilate until your fingers tingle.

Low oxygen (hypoxia) develops insidiously; unconsciousness may sneak up on the diver before he is aware of any problem. Scuba divers do not suffer from breathhold hyperventilation, but they occasionally may have problems with oxygen supply. Hypoxia does not develop if a properly filled air tank is correctly used. Mistakes have been made so that tanks were filled with gases other than air. Very corroded tanks can have internal oxygen consumption by corrosion. Closed or semiclosed scuba presents a risk of hypoxia and this is one reason these rigs are not suitable for recreational diving.

At very high levels carbon dioxide causes unconsciousness. However, other problems usually intervene before carbon dioxide reaches these levels. Skin divers will not have dangerously elevated carbon dioxide. Rebreathing scuba apparatus frequently malfunctions to cause carbon dioxide accumulation. A properly used open circuit scuba vents exhaled air and thus eliminates carbon dioxide. Most divers will not have elevated carbon dioxide even with a moderate amount of "skip breathing." Some highly trained divers appear to retain carbon dioxide and this has been implicated as a possible cause of injury.

Nitrogen narcosis, in its severe stages, causes unconsciousness and drowning. Milder forms may lead to drowning through irrational behavior. Nitrogen narcosis is discussed in detail in chapter 14.

Air from poor sources may have high carbon monoxide concentrations. Carbon monoxide results in tissue hypoxia and in unconsciousness. Reputable air suppliers monitor their equipment to ensure its purity. Two common sources of contamination are from high temperatures in oil lubricated compressors or from improper exhausting of gasoline compressor engines.

The body depends on the regular, rhythmic contractions of the heart for its blood supply. Disruptions in this rhythm, known as arrhythmias, may interfere with circulation. Fainting results when the blood supply to the brain is even momentarily interrupted. Arrhythmias occur in many forms. Many of them are common and not necessarily hazardous. Others quickly kill. Victims of heart attack die most frequently from arrhythmias.

Breathhold diving has been repeatedly shown to have a fairly high associated incidence of arrhythmias. Fortunately these are almost always of the harmless type. A diver with heart disease, however, may lose consciousness from an arrhythmia. Elevated carbon dioxide frequently causes arrhythmias and this has been suggested as the cause of some drownings. Diagnosis of most arrhythmias requires an electrocardiogram.

Air embolism and decompression sickness can kill through unconsciousness and drowning. Indeed, unconsciousness is the most common sign of air embolism. Recreational divers rarely have the sudden, catastrophic type of decompression sickness which causes unconsciousness in the water. It is more characteristic of "blow ups" in commercial diving.

Prevention of Drowning

A tragically large percentage of drownings would have been prevented by adherence to the most basic diving principles. These principles concern diver selection, education, and practice. Diver selection has been discussed and is very important in prevention of drowning. Physically and mentally fit divers are more able to tolerate the vicissitude of the sea without becoming exhausted or panicked. The healthy diver is less likely to suffer from an incapacitating illness.

Diver education requires attention to developing skills which make a person safe and comfortable in the water. The student needs to learn how to avoid problems and how to react when they occur. Obviously, this education requires work in the water.

For both trainees and graduates, it is the actual techniques used, rather than theories known, that define safe divers. Most divers know "the rules," but sometimes choose to ignore them. Even in classes, unsafe practices abound. Over ten percent of diving fatalities happen during class dives. This is amazing considering the supervision that should be provided.

The following is a list of basic diving principles for students and certified divers.

a. Do not dive when feeling ill.

b. Do not dive under the influence of alcohol or debilitating drugs.

c. Medicines must be evaluated before use when diving.

d. Maintain proper diving fitness.

e. Do not dive alone.

f. Dive only with adequate, well maintained equipment.

g. Evaluate conditions before diving: storms, currents, surf, condition of the sea, and entanglements.

h. Remember that specialty diving requires specialty training.

Adhering to the first four principles greatly reduces the chances of getting into trouble. If trouble does come knocking on your door, these principles will increase your chances of survival. Do not be like the Navy scuba diver who drowned in a calm river while using a buddy line. Autopsy showed he had begun the dive while suffering from severe bilateral pneumonia.

Proper equipment reduces the likelihood of an accident. Proper does not mean excessive equipment. An easy to use flotation device is essential. Naturally, the wet suited diver will float if he drops weights. But a safety vest should still be used. A simple vest can keep the exhausted diver safely above water, but vests that float the user face down do not help much.

Safe diving requires careful planning. Match the divers to the situation. Rough seas not only diminish fun, they also increase the possibility of accidents. Fighting the ocean only leads to exhaustion.

Diving skills increase gradually. The new diver is not ready for rough water diving. Similarly, he is not ready for specialty diving in caves, wrecks, or ice. These rewarding activities require special techniques and equipment. Approximately twenty percent of diving deaths in the U.S. occur in cave diving.

No one should be taught that diving alone is smart, or safe. More than half of the fatalities in skin diving happen in solo diving and almost fifteen percent of scuba deaths are in solitary diving. Of course, having a buddy does not guarantee his presence. Buddies get separated and then it is like diving alone. A properly functioning buddy system prevents many accidents by making assistance available. The system also diminishes the seriousness of accidents by making prompt rescue possible.

RESCUES

Despite proper diving, accidents do plague divers. The result of an accident depends on the behavior of the victim and his fellow divers. Diving fosters independence—one of its most appealing features. An injured diver relies on his skills and those of his buddies. Only after the initial rescue will other people be involved. Waiting for a professional rescuer usually means too long a wait. Therefore, every diver needs to know basic rescue techniques.

Arguments rage that the introductory scuba class is no place to teach lifesaving. But where will the student learn? Standard lifesaving courses are useful, but have limited application to diving. After all, how many divers carry a life ring?

Diving rescue and lifesaving are basic, not advanced, skills and should be part of every diver's education. As witnessed by the incidence of accidents during diving instruction, rescue skills cannot be considered an optional subject, or one for advanced classes. Instruction involves lectures, pool work, and supervised open water practice. This section introduces the subject but cannot substitute for actual practice.

Rescues may begin underwater or on the surface. Obviously, a successful rescue ends above water regardless of its starting point. Some victims will be breathing, others will not. Management depends very much on ventilatory condition. Rescue of the unconscious diver differs from that of the conscious diver.

Starting the Rescue

Rescues start with the realization that a diver needs help. The rescuer may be summoned by the victim or may make the observation himself. This initial step seems simple, but it is one of the major causes of failed rescues. A successful rescue depends on a properly executed sequence of maneuvers. Failure at any step dooms the whole rescue.

Too many accidents end with the appraisal, "We did everything right except . . . " The rescuer notes the need for assistance and goes quickly to help. Delay can easily turn a minor mishap into a drowning. The conscious, exhausted diver may lose consciousness and sink, and the unconscious diver may suffer respiratory and cardiac failure.

Contact with the victim moves the rescue into the next phase. Delays in reaching victims are very common. Among skin diving fatalities, recovery of the victim took more than ten minutes in sixty percent of the cases. Scuba results are better, but recovery still took more than ten minutes in forty percent of fatal accidents. A victim may be very quickly lost.

In the case of an apprehensive diver, visual and vocal contact may be sufficient to correct the situation. Reassurance may enable the diver to avoid panic and to continue safely. In most cases the victim should be encouraged to end the dive since the problem may recur. This would not apply if the precipitating event was relatively minor, such as a flooded snorkel. Never let a buddy or group member go ashore alone. Many fatalities take place from this type of poor judgment.

Extreme caution must be taken in approaching the frightened, struggling diver. All life saving courses teach that an accident may claim two lives if the rescuer carelessly swims within reach of the victim. Push a surf mat or other float to the victim. Talk to him and tell him to drop his weights and to inflate his vest. A surprisingly large number of divers in trouble never think to do this. If the victim continues in distress, actual bodily contact becomes necessary. But do not swim right into the victim's arms. Approach from behind, preferably underwater, and use a lifesaving hold to keep the victim from getting free to embrace you.

Underwater Rescues

Divers needing rescue underwater are more likely to be unconscious, since the conscious diver generally struggles to the surface by instinct. Of course, a minor mishap may take place which can be solved by reassuringly guiding the diver to the surface to evaluate the situation. A trapped or entangled diver may be found before consciousness is lost. Care must be taken to avoid getting yourself trapped or entangled. The struggling underwater victim should be approached carefully to prevent panicked grabbing.

Do not put yourself in an extremely dangerous position in a desperate attempt to make a rescue. A diver in Monterey, California went to the assistance of a companion who was in trouble while making a deep dive. Both divers succumbed to nitrogen narcosis and drowned. Sometimes this is a difficult and painful decision, but the amateur rescuer should not take foolhardy chances.

The unconscious victim must be brought to the surface. Do not waste time checking for breathing or pulses. There is no way to perform effective resuscitation underwater. Ditch the victim's weights as this makes your ascent much easier. Small vests may be inflated but large vests in shallow water may provide too much lift for an orderly ascent. Adjust your buoyancy as necessary. If possible, keep your weights as you might need them to make another dive. Ascent should be efficient, but not overly fast as this can result in decompression sickness or embolism. Be sure that you breathe normally.

If the victim is breathing and still holding the regulator, the chance of embolism or drowning is reduced. The unconscious, non-breathing scuba victim requires a decision. Decide if effort should be made to compress the chest to force out air during ascent, or if there is a better position for ascent. An unconscious victim quickly becomes hypoxic and the vocal cords relax. Expanding air will freely pass out of the lungs. Head up is the simplest position. Attempts to open the airway by head position usually take more time than they are worth because air escape is rarely a problem in the unconscious victim. Time is much more important. Get the victim to the surface.

Transport

By now contact has been made with the victim and submerged victims have been brought to the surface. If the victim is not breathing, mouth-to-mouth resuscitation must begin immediately. A conscious diver will be breathing.

All rescues must move toward shore or another refuge. If the victim requires artificial resuscitation, a speedy trip is essential. When time permits, signal for help. A whistle worn on the vest may prove handy for this purpose.

The victim can be carried in any number of ways. Buoyancy is essential and can be provided by ditching weights, inflating the vest, and using a mat or board. Do not use a carry technique which results in the victim being pushed underwater. Transport is easier when there are helpers to push and pull.

Remember to keep conscious victims under control to prevent panicked grasping. Never lose contact with the victim. Many divers are lost during the trip to shore. The maintenance of contact may be difficult in rough seas. The biggest problem arises at the surf line. In very heavy surf you have to wait offshore until a boat or helicopter can reach you. This delay is unfortunate but sometimes advisable if such a passage would likely result in injury to the rescuers or loss of the victim. You can afford longer delays with a spontaneously breathing victim. Do not delay unduly as fatigue and chilling develop quickly.

The rescue does not end with delivering the victim to the beach or boat. Once ashore, check him for breathing and pulse and then follow the first aid principles discussed in chapter 5. Failure here means failure of the entire rescue.

Resuscitation

The body requires an uninterrupted supply of oxygen. In drowning, impaired ventilatory function interferes with oxygen supply and this impairs heart function. Death follows from respiratory and/or cardiac arrest. As the English physiologist Haldane so aptly put it, "Lack of oxygen not only stops the body's machinery, it wrecks the machine."

A person begins to die when oxygen supply to the brain ceases. Immediately, consciousness is lost. With the passage of time, brain cells begin to die. Irreversible brain damage takes place before death. Many factors modify the brain's tolerance to anoxia (no oxygen) but in general, permanent damage occurs after five to six minutes.

In most drownings ventilation fails before the heart. The time interval from ventilatory arrest to cardiac arrest varies widely but is generally only a few minutes. During this interval, restoring ventilation can prevent cardiac arrest. Occasionally the heart arrests before breathing stops. Breathing will then stop very soon. It is important to realize that drowning proceeds in a continuum from normalcy to death. Death from drowning is not sudden. Prompt, effective action can stop the process early before permanent damage takes place. Delayed action makes resuscitation more difficult and increases the chances of residual injury. No definite time limits can be given because of the many modifying factors. Just remember the damage is time dependent. Any savings in time improves chances for survival.

The Diving Reflex and Prolonged Survival

In general, only a few minutes of immersion cause drownings. However, there are several cases of persons who have survived immersions of as long as forty minutes. The explanation may be based partially on the diving reflex.

This reflex, seen in man and diving animals, causes a slowing of the heart and shifting of blood flow in response to the stimulus of skin contact with water. Blood flow shifts away from skin and muscles to the vital organs. These changes markedly reduce oxygen consumption and increase breathhold time. The reflex also includes inhibition of breathing so the victim tends not to inhale as much water as expected during immersion. Facial stimuli are more powerful than other parts of the body. Breathing with a snorkel or scuba markedly reduces the reflex's potency.

The diving reflex alone would not explain survival after prolonged submergence. All the cases have happened in very cold water, many in near freezing temperatures. Profound cold augments the diving reflex. It also directly reduces oxygen consumption. However, moderately cold water increases oxygen consumption and reduces tolerable immersion time.

The diving reflex is not a complete blessing. Profound heart slowing may cause fatal cardiac arrhythmias.

It is rare for people to survive prolonged immersion. Do not use this phenomenon to make excuses for delayed rescues and resuscitations. But, do not arbitrarily abandon hope if the rescue is delayed.

Techniques of Resuscitation

Timing is of utmost importance in resuscitation. As previously discussed the passage of time greatly reduces the chance of a successful resuscitation. Cardiac arrest victims fared better when resuscitation was begun by trained laymen than a similar group whose resuscitation awaited the arrival of a rescue squad. In diving

Mouth-to-mouth resuscitation on the beach

it is not feasible to expect prompt assistance from a rescue team. It has been estimated that just delaying resuscitation until reaching shore would kill almost fifty percent of near-drowning victims.

If you intend to dive in open water, you should know how to administer *cardiopulmonary resuscitation* (CPR). The prudent diver makes certain that his buddy is also trained in CPR. Most diving instructors are not CPR instructors but instruction is readily available through the Red Cross, American Heart Association, and some municipal programs. A very basic course may take only three hours. The techniques must be practiced on mannequins, not just read about. Resuscitation in the water is far different than on land so there should be water practice sessions. Diving rescue workshops have proven useful in teaching rescues and resuscitation to large groups of divers.

First aid CPR techniques have been quite standarized and this assists education. However, it is the result, rather than blind adherence to a pattern, that really matters. The goal of CPR is to support life until the body recovers spontaneously or until more definitive therapy can be provided. Life is supported by ventilating the victim's lungs and by supporting circulation when necessary. CPR does not duplicate normal physiology: mouth-to-mouth breathing provides only sixteen percent oxygen compared to twenty-one percent in normal breathing. Cardiac compression gives a cardiac output only twenty-five percent of normal. This means the margin for error is very small. Start promptly and proceed properly and continuously.

Resuscitation cannot be done underwater so the starting point is always on the surface. Remember that a conscious victim is breathing. Upon contacting an unconscious diver, get his head up out of the water. Tilting the head back usually opens the air way.

The standard rule for ascertaining the presence of breathing is to look for chest movement and to feel and listen for the air movement. These steps may admittedly be difficult in the water. If there is any doubt, begin artificial ventilation by sealing the nose with one hand and giving four quick breaths into the victim's mouth. (There is nothing magical about four quick breaths. It could just as well be three or five.) Your pauses for inhalation between breaths should be very brief. Watch the victim's chest to be sure you are getting air into the lungs (the chest should rise as you ventilate). The most common failure in CPR is in not getting sufficient air into the lungs. The purpose of four quick breaths is to provide rapid reoxygenation. This may prevent cardiac arrest or even restore cardiac function if the heart has just stopped.

Mouth-to-mouth is not easy in the water. Obviously, the masks of both victim and rescuer must be removed. It is almost impossible to keep the victim's head up without artificial buoyancy which can be provided by inflating his vest. After the first four breaths, a few moments can be taken to improve buoyancy, but then try to maintain a breathing rate of twelve per minute during the swim to shore.

A popular carry called the "do-ce-do" (after the square dance maneuver) provides good contact and gets the victim's head up for ventilation *(see photograph).* Do not climb up on the victim as this pushes him underwater. Some people recognize the difficulty of ventilation in the water and suggest four quick breaths and full speed to shore without further in-water resuscitation. Unfortunately, the benefits of the oxygen depleted breaths will be lost before shore is reached in most cases. Admittedly ventilation is difficult, but the effort is justified. We are not dealing with ideal solutions. We are trying to improve on a very poor situation.

Dry land demonstration of "Do-Ce-Do" position

Particularly in the east, there is some interest in using a snorkel tube for ventilation instead of continuing mouth-to-mouth. This has the advantage of not pushing the victim underwater. The proponents like it in rough water; the critics do not. The biggest disadvantage is that it requires a piece of equipment which is not always handy. Getting set up may take too long. Snorkel rescue breathing is feasible but requires special training.

Crossing the surf line may be very difficult. This is the only time when it may be advisable to stop ventilation briefly. But keep the interruption to the absolute minimum.

Cardiac Resuscitation

In most drownings, breathing fails before the heart fails. Mouth-to-mouth resuscitation may keep the heart going. If cardiac arrest occurs, external cardiac massage is necessary. Unfortunately, there is not an effective way to perform cardiac massage in the water. Therefore, it does not make sense to waste time in the water deciding if a cardiac arrest has happened. With cold hands and a cold, suited victim, determination of heart activity is indeed difficult. Begin mouth-to-mouth and evaluate cardiac function once the shore is reached.

Continue mouth-to-mouth ventilation and feel for a pulse. In a suited diver the most accessible pulse is from the carotid artery. (There is one on each side of the neck.) Push gently on one, never both, and feel for a pulse, removing your gloves first. Pulses will be absent in cardiac arrest. Cardiac arrest is now used not only to mean stopping of the heart; it also refers to venticular fibrillation which is non-functional, uncoordinated contracting of heart muscle fibers. If there is no pulse, begin cardiac compression.

Cardiac compression is dangerous if improperly performed. Ribs can be easily fractured and may tear vital organs. The incidence of fractured ribs has been high in those deceased divers who received CPR by non-professionals. When properly performed CPR does not fracture ribs. As you do cardiac compression, don't be rushed into sloppy technique. The basic steps are listed here, but you need formal training in CPR if you expect to be any good.

a. Victim must be supine on a firm surface.

b. Kneel beside victim.

c. Measure two fingers breadth up from tip of the breast bone or sternum.

d. The heel of one hand is placed over the sternum with the other hand on top. Keep the fingers off the ribs.

e. Lean over the victim and with the arms straight, rock forward so that the hands force the sternum down one and one half to two inches.

f. Rock quickly back and release pressure without removing hands from the sternum.

g. Repeat at a rate of sixty compressions per minute.

Artificial ventilation must continue during chest compression. With two rescuers, twelve breaths per minute can be interposed with the sixty compressions. One rescuer can provide CPR but will be quickly fatigued. A solo CPR gives two breaths then fifteen compressions in each cycle. The chest compression should give a palpable pulse to the carotid artery. Usually chest compression is adequate in degree but frequently is too slow.

Once you have begun CPR do not stop until relieved by professional rescuers. Someone in your diving party should quickly call the local emergency facility to summon help. If your diving equipment includes oxygen and a method of administration, the chances of resuscitation are improved. Pure oxygen is superior to expired air. Oxygen can be given with a self-inflating bag and mask or with a mask and ventilating valve. The use of this equipment requires advanced training. Above all, do not delay resuscitation while awaiting specialized equipment or personnel.

Near drowning victims often swallow a lot of water. This characteristically results in vomiting during transportation and on the beach. The mouth should be cleaned as necessary but do not waste much time doing it. Efforts to drain the victim are usually non-productive and take too long. Laying the victim with his head toward the ocean utilizes the beach's natural slope to promote drainage from the mouth and to improve blood return to the chest and to the brain.

Follow-Up Care

First aid of the nearly drowned must be followed by medical evaluation. Only a very minor accident, such as a surf tumble, can be ignored. Patients may be revived and conscious, then die from the effects of prolonged hypoxia. Physicians dealing with near drownings know that consciousness and normal chest X-rays do not mean the damage is slight. Intensive care of the near drowned has greatly improved the survival rate.

Today the major limitation to survival starts at the accident site. Victims who reach emergency rooms after prompt resuscitation will survive when given intensive hospital care. Those victims who reach the hospital without pulses or ventilation usually die or suffer permanent damage. Full recovery occurs in only one percent of these patients despite the best hospital care.

7

Barotrauma on Descent

The waters of Hawaii quickly make a diver forget the ordeal of cold, rough, visionless diving. A moderately experienced scuba diver began a leisurely descent off Pokai Bay only to be stopped by a familiar pain in his right ear. He squeezed his nose, exhaled, felt a "pop" and kept on going down to forty feet.

Below him at about sixty feet, a handsome helmet shell was leaving its unmistakable track in the sand. The diver saw the animal just moments before the ear pain returned. This time the nose squeeze routine did not help. He followed the animal for almost ten minutes, stuck at forty feet. Then the words of his instructor came back to him. "Sometimes," he had said, "you may find it necessary to ascend a few feet, clear there, and then go down again." Ten feet up the diver felt his ear clear and then he made a direct descent to visit the helmet shell.

You can avoid a lot of problems by diving in the clear waters of Hawaii, but you cannot escape the nemesis of pressure.

The high density of water results in rapidly increasing pressure with depth. Our whole earthly, gaseous atmosphere only exerts 14.7 pounds per square inch. An ocean dive to just about thirty-three feet adds pressure equivalent to this atmosphere. Thus, the pressure at thirty-three feet can be called two atmospheres. Each subsequent thirty-three feet adds another atmosphere (0.445 pounds per square inch/foot of depth). Hence, total pressure on the body increases impressively during even a modest dive.

At thirty-three feet an average sized person will have 82,000 pounds pushing on his body. Fortunately, this pressure causes no problems to most of the body. It is simply transmitted through the solids and liquids which comprise the vast majority of the tissues. Only the air containing spaces are affected by pressure changes. Pressure damages to tissues is called *barotrauma*. The

65

more common word "squeeze" nicely describes what happens on the descent part of a dive. But barotrauma also occurs on ascent when water pressure decreases. (*See chapter* 8.)

The body has two basic types of air spaces. Some, like the middle ear, have rigid walls, while others have distensible walls such as the gut. Rigid wall spaces react quickly to pressure changes. Fully distensible spaces harmlessly expand or contract. Unfortunately, the lungs are a modified distensible space with limited capacity for compression or expansion.

MIDDLE EAR BAROTRAUMA

A person does not have to be much of a diver to experience the most common form of descent barotrauma—ear squeeze. Ear pain can occur in three feet of water and actual tympanic membrane damage requires less than five feet of water.

The middle ear is a small space between the tympanic membrane (eardrum) and the inner ear. The middle ear contains the three bones which conduct sound impulses from the tympanic membrane to the oval window and then to hearing organs of the inner ear.

On descent, water pressure pushes in on the tympanic membrane. Pressure transmitted to the lining tissues of the middle ear causes the lining membrane to bulge into the middle ear. These inward forces cause pain and then transudation of fluid into the middle ear. The small blood vessels in the lining and in the tympanic membrane can rupture. Eventually distension of the tympanic membrane causes it to rupture.

Fortunately damage from middle ear barotrauma is usually mild because most divers abandon the dive when pain occurs. A squeezed ear may cause some temporary hearing impairment. Occasionally, marked pressure differentials may disrupt the stapes' (part of the middle ear) connection with the oval window and cause dizziness or hearing loss. Actual rupture of the oval window or the round window, the other window to the inner ear, has occurred with resulting dizziness or deafness. Water in the middle ear upsets balance and dirty water may lead to ear infections.

Middle ear barotrauma can be avoided by ventilating the ear through the eustachian tube. This tiny tube which passes up from the rear of the pharynx to the middle ear can be voluntarily opened to admit air which offsets the inward thrust of the tympanic membrane and the ear lining. This equalizing of pressure is commonly called "clearing the ears."

People vary widely in their ability to "clear." Some can open their eustachian tubes with only a swallow or a slight movement of the jaw. Others struggle and may never be successful. In groups of otherwise fit diving candidates the most common cause of dropout is ear problems. Three major categories of problems prevent clearing. They include:

a. Not knowing how to properly equalize.

b. Episodic illnesses which prevent eustachian tube opening.

c. Anatomical abnormalities which prevent proper ear ventilation. (A few people have deformities, congenital or from disease, which restrict their eustachian tube function.)

A diver could find out which category his problem falls into by consulting an otolaryngologist (ear specialist).

The first step in clearing the ears is preparation. Upper respiratory infections or allergies ("hayfever") may temporarily make the eustachian tubes non-functional. Ideally diving should be postponed until the condition has resolved.

Drugs can be used, but these may be ineffective or even dangerous. The decongestant sprays and pills usually contain either antihistamines or symphomimetic drugs. Many "cold" medicines contain both these drugs. Antihistamines often cause drowsiness which obviously makes them dangerous for divers. The symphomimetic drugs stimulate the autonomic nervous system. In some persons this results in blood pressure elevation and rapid pulse rate. Most decongestants have a "rebound" action. After several days of use they worsen rather than relieve congestion.

Most divers occasionally use a decongestant. Decongestants should be chosen by following a few simple principles. Do not just pick a decongestant off a shelf and use it for diving. Get your physician's advice and be sure he knows you will be using it while diving, which requires utmost alertness. Try out the medicine on a non-diving day. Verify that it does not sedate you. Use the medicine only once in a while. A chronic problem requires medical attention. Finally, do not expect a drug to solve all your ear problems.

Preparation includes learning the techniques of ear equalization. Much of this learning can be done by land practice. Every diver has to equalize his ears. Do not be fooled by tales of old pros who go down without clearing. Even the pros have to clear—they just do it more efficiently and effortlessly than the neophyte. Practice definitely does help. Often an experienced diver can clear almost automatically even if his early diving was difficult.

There are numerous ways of opening the eustachian tubes. Perhaps the simplest is swallowing as done when flying. Related techniques include moving the jaw from side to side, trying to wiggle the ears, or yawning. Pinching the nose shut and exhaling is often the most effective equalizing technique. When done gently, it is an excellent method.

Straining against a shut nose and mouth—the Valsalva maneuver—opens ears, but may be hazardous. The high pressures generated affect blood pressure and heart action. Pressure in the middle ear, transmitted through the skull to the inner ear, can damage the ear bones, oval and round windows, and the organs of hearing and balance. A diver who one day needs a hard Valsalva should spend that day reading diving equipment catalogs. A diver who never can clear without a hard Valsalva needs retraining and perhaps reevaluation by a physician.

The following statement reflects a common misunderstanding. A student reports, "I get down about ten feet, have real pain and just can't clear my ears."

Equalizing *must* begin *before* ten feet. As noted earlier, ear damage happens in very shallow water. Water pressure increases linearly but the relative effects are greater in the early part of the descent. The Hawaiian diver who got stuck at forty feet is not typical. Usually, successful clearing to thirty-three feet means the rest of the dive will be easy. Start to clear early, don't wait for pain.

The eustachian tubes actually lock shut at pressure differentials of about ninety millimeters mercury—less than five feet of sea water. It appears that part of the tubes collapse at these pressures. Then, even the most vigorous effort will not open the eustachian tubes. When clearing is impossible, an ascent of a few feet may sufficiently reduce pressure to make tube opening possible.

Position in the water affects ease of ear equalization. Lying flat, as in swimming, or with the head down—a typical descent—limits tube opening by increasing pressure on the tube. Stopping and assuming an upright position may make clearing possible.

Treatment of Barotrauma

Most cases of middle ear barotrauma require no treatment. In fact the usual case of mild pain resolves with no symptoms persisting after the dive. If a diver fails to heed the warning pain, there may be damage to the tympanic membrane, middle ear, or inner ear. Evidence of injury would include bleeding from the ear canal, deafness, ringing in the ear (tinnitus), or dizziness.

See a physician promptly if these signs occur. Treatment involves cessation of diving until healing. Some medication may be prescribed, but other injuries may require surgery. Severe injury may make any future diving inadvisable. Divers must realize that prevention surpasses therapy.

OTHER FORMS OF BAROTRAUMA

Even today an occasional misguided diver tries to use ear plugs. A tightly fitting plug forms an air space in the canal. During a dive the lining tissues of the canal will be damaged in a fashion similar to middle ear squeeze. If the diver equalizes his middle ear, the tympanic membrane will bulge out into the low pressure of the ear canal. Simultaneously, water pressure pushes the plug deeper into the canal. It may become tightly wedged and difficult to remove. There is no right way to use ear plugs in diving.

Misfit suit hoods can block the ear canal and cause difficulties similar to those from ear plugs. Both dry and wet suit hoods must not be allowed to fit so tightly that canal air or water circulation is blocked. Some divers cut ear holes in their wet suit hoods, but this is not necessary with a properly fitted suit.

The Sinuses. The paranasal sinuses (frontal, maxillary, sphenoid, and ethmoid) are air cavities of the face which communicate with the nose. When the sinus ducts are open, pressure equalization occurs. This is automatic during a dive. Blockage of a duct causes problems similar to middle ear barotrauma. A relative vacuum forms in the sinus, resulting in blood vessel engorgement within the lining membrane. Transudation and then bleeding follows if the dive continues. In almost all cases pain accompanies sinus squeeze but a significant number of divers have painless sinus bleeding. The blood from the sinuses eventually comes out the nose and over half the cases of sinus barotrauma result in epistaxsis (bleeding from the nose). Fortunately, sinus squeeze is much less common than middle ear squeeze (about two percent in a large group of diving trainees).

There is no voluntary technique to clear a blocked sinus during a dive. Upper respiratory infections and allergies lead the causes of duct obstruction. Other reasons for blocked sinuses include nasal septum deviation and nasal polyps.

Decongestant sprays and pills have the same use and disadvantage as in middle ear squeeze. Repeated sinus squeeze makes diving difficult and unpleasant. An otolaryngologist could investigate the factors which cause the squeeze. Most sinus squeeze resolves spontaneously but sinus infections have occurred.

Lung Barotrauma. In scuba diving the inhalation of high pressure air automatically equalizes pressures between the lungs and the water. The breath-hold diver's lungs compress as outside water pressure pushes in on the chest wall and shifts the abdominal organs up against the diaphragm. In the usual skin dive this causes no difficulties since the lungs are quite distensible. Eventually the lungs can be compressed to a point where they lose their distensibility and begin to act like a rigid air space. Diving beyond this depth causes transudation of fluid and bleeding into the lungs. Lung (or thoracic) squeeze may cause permanent damage. Very few skin divers dive deep enough for lung squeeze. The threshold varies from individual to individual. The lungs become noncompressible at their residual volume. After a maximum exhalation, one to three liters of air still remain in the lungs. This is known as the residual volume.

At the beginning of a breath-hold dive, forceful inhalation brings lung volume to total lung capacity—the individual's maximum lung volume. This may range from four to six liters. Water pressure compresses this volume linearly. Thus at thirty-three feet lung volume would be three liters in a diver with a lung capacity of six liters. This diver would reach residual volume (assume it is one and one-half liters) at ninety-nine feet. But, of course, few skin divers get near ninety-nine feet. Inhalation to only half lung capacity would reduce lung volume to residual at a much shallower depth. Training extends breath-hold depth limits by increasing total lung capacity and decreasing residual volume.

Diving too deep makes the chest hurt as it compresses. This should be a warning sign to stop the descent. A seriously injured diver may have difficulty upon surfacing. Frothy blood-tinged fluid may be coughed up. Prompt evaluation by a physician is essential. Oxygen should be breathed, if available.

Another change is physiology extends the depth threshold. Immersion causes blood volume in the chest to expand. The blood comes there from other parts of the body. Putting a non-compressible fluid into the chest compresses air, thus reducing residual air volume. This mechanism largely explains why world diving records exceed theoretical limits based on surface determination of lung volumes.

Lung squeeze is a rare form of descent barotrauma. But its seriousness makes prevention essential. There is no specific form of therapy and fatalities have been reported.

Other Forms. When you dive you notice that your mask pushes in on your face as you descend. The mask creates an artificial, rigid air space. A short nasal exhalation relieves this snugness. Failure to exhale into the mask causes mask (or face) squeeze. Small blood vessels in the face and eyes can be broken in facial barotrauma. Swimming goggles are dangerous in diving because there is no way to equalize the air space in them to water (and tissue) pressure.

Poorly fit dry suits can trap folds of skin in air pockets and can cause skin barotrauma. As mentioned above, a wet suit hood can occasionally cause air trapping in the ear canal.

Rarely, tooth squeeze occurs from air pockets in careous or inadequately repaired teeth.

8

Barotrauma on Ascent

After a stormy winter the calm Pacific appeared especially inviting to the Nathanville recreation department scuba class. Dick especially looked forward to that day's dive. A "C" card depended on this day so he had no intention of letting a little head cold stop him. After a surf entry the plan called for a gradual descent to forty feet and then an underwater swim through the kelp forest with a concluding rocky exit.

Dick made a slow descent because his ears really hurt. At one point the assistant instructor almost made him quit but Dick finally forced his way down. Then everything went well until time to come up. On ascent his ears hurt again. With great effort he cleared them but then the sinus pain began and never really quit all the way up. It was hours after the dive before he felt normal.

The person the class remembered most after the dive was Harry. Harry did not like the surf entry; it scared him and was hard work. By the time he headed down into the dark water his self confidence was virtually gone. Usually, a kelp forest in reasonably clear water is beautiful, but Harry found the limited visibility and strangeness made the dive a horror. His leg knife caught on a stalk. He reached down to free himself and began to swim on when his dangling pressure gauge got tangled. He jerked it free but then the regulator mouthpiece slipped from his mouth. Weeks of training were forgotten. Harry kicked his way wildly to the surface with his regulator trailing behind.

When the instructor reached the surface, Harry was lying motionless. The instructor remained calm as he verified that Harry was breathing and then towed him to shore. Harry regained consciousness in a pressure chamber four hundred miles from the checkout site.

Dick and Harry are two extreme examples of *ascent baro-trauma*. On descent, water pressure squeezes air spaces and on ascent these spaces expand. Expanding air may affect the ears, sinuses, or lungs. Results of ascent barotrauma range from inconvenient to catastrophic.

The Ears. Normally the eustachian tube opens automatically when middle ear pressure increases. This eliminates the need to manually "clear" the ears. Occasionally the tube does not open and the expanding air pushes the tympanic membrane outward. The inner ear windows will also be distended.

Uneven pressure equalization may cause the vertigo sometimes present during ascent. When the eustachian tubes do not open automatically it may be necessary to "clear" them using the same techniques employed for descent. Allergies or infections which make descent difficult may also impair ascent. This is another reason to postpone diving when equalizing may be difficult. Dick, for example, should have put off his dive to another time, thus avoiding "squeeze."

The Sinuses. Ascent barotrauma is more common in the sinuses than in the ears. It occurs about half as often as descent sinus barotrauma. Sometimes the occlusion of the sinus acts like a ball valve or flutter valve to permit air entry during descent while inhibiting its egress on ascent. Pain is the most common symptom, but twenty-five percent of the cases may have nasal bleeding without pain.

The Lungs. Lung barotrauma, such as suffered by Harry, is not as common but it ranks second to drowning as the cause of death in scuba accidents. Lung barotrauma can kill directly or lead to drowning. Ascent lung injuries result from overexpansion of the lung tissue with subsequent rupture.

Skin divers do not rupture their lungs, because on ascent the lungs can expand only back to their original size—minus the volume of oxygen removed.

The scuba diver has a constant source of air so his lungs are not compressed. When he ascends, the gas in his lungs expands and is exhaled into the water. If a scuba diver takes a breath and fails to exhale during ascent, the lungs expand. Though distensible, the lungs will rupture if the expansion continues. Lung rupture has resulted in fatalities in only nine feet of fresh water.

Failure to exhale on ascent and overexpansion despite exhalation are the two basic mechanisms that cause lung overexpansion.

Failure to exhale usually involves a panicked ascent or may be caused by running out of air and ascending improperly. The rational diver will not hold his breath during an ascent as increasing lung pressure will remind him to exhale. But a panicked diver may either ignore this signal or ascend so fast that the crucial expansion occurs without warning. A big buoyancy compensator can give a rapid ride to the surface. Ascent rates in Navy buoyant submarine escapes are five and one half feet per second. Not much time for orderly thinking, especially if this is combined with fear.

The otherwise intelligent scuba diver who "skip breathes" may rupture his lungs by changing depth while breathholding. A diver does not have to come all the way to the surface in order to rupture a lung.

Some lung ruptures have developed even though the victim appeared to have exhaled normally. This is difficult to verify in scuba accidents because continual rather than continuous breathing may be at fault. However, there are verified cases of rupture with continuous exhalation. Despite exhalation, limited areas of the lung may not expel their air.

These localized areas of trapped air expand and can rupture. The blockage may be one way that permits inhalation but retards exhalation. Obstruction may come from stones, scars, or plugs of mucus. Weakened air passages seen in asthma and emphysema may collapse during exhalation. Older people (past mid-40s) may have some closed airways during normal breathing.

Recently it has been shown that water immersion increases air trapping. This seems to result from the smaller lung volumes secondary to chest compression and to blood shifts into the chest. Some physicians have theorized that this process may cause overexpansion after forceful exhalation during the early stages of emergency ascents. However, these theories fail to recognize that on ascent the trapped air will expand and tend to force open the functionally closed airways. In normal lungs this pathway would offer the least resistance to expanding air and would relieve pressure on lung walls. In abnormal lungs rupture might happen.

Gas exchange in the lungs occurs in the tiny alveoli (air sacs). These alveoli are the sites of rupture in lung barotrauma. When an alveolus ruptures, air escapes causing interstitial emphysema. The air usually passes to the mediastinum: the space in the middle of the chest which contains the heart, trachea, and esophagus. Air in the mediastinum (mediastinal emphysema) can pass up under the skin of the chest and the neck to form subcutaneous emphysema. Mediastinal air can also dissect out between the pleural linings which cover the surface of the lung. Air in the pleural space causes lung collapse (pneumothorax). If an alveolus lying on the lung surface ruptures, air can directly enter the pleural space to cause pneumothorax. More commonly, however, air moves out from the mediastinum to the pleural space.

If a violent alveolar injury tears the surrounding capillaries, air enters the blood stream. This air forms emboli that go to the left side of the heart and are then pumped out the aorta. Most typically, the air emboli go into the brain's circulation but, not infrequently, these bubbles enter the coronary arteries which nourish the heart.

The lungs may rupture at any stage of ascent. Ascent after rupture causes the escaped air to expand and worsens the damage. Usually the air leak stops soon after reaching the surface although it may persist. The results of lung rupture range from no symptoms to death. In a careful X-ray study, one percent of submarine escape trainees had evidence of lung rupture without any symptoms. Mediastinal and subcutaneous emphysema are generally not very serious but the air can cause obstruction to breathing and interfere with the circulation.

A large pneumothorax may seriously impair breathing. Air embolism is the widely recognized serious complication of lung rupture. In submarine escape training seventy-three percent of all lung ruptures caused air embolism. Air embolism causes damage by obstruction of blood flow in the brain and to the heart.

Understanding Lung Rupture

It is important to identify promptly the occurrence of lung rupture. Three basic principles apply to lung overexpansion accidents. First, they occur with scuba, not with breathhold diving. Second, they can happen in very shallow water ascents, and third, symptoms usually appear soon after surfacing (in contrast with decompression sickness). Mediastinal and subcutaneous emphysema symptoms may have more gradual onset.

Each form of injury has typical signs. Some of the symptoms are explained here.

Mediastinal emphysema. Usually no symptoms if it occurs by itself, or a crunching sound may be heard with a stethescope. Mediastinal emphysema may cause mid-chest pain or difficult inspiration, but it rarely affects heart function.

Subcutaneous emphysema. Skin of neck swells up and has a crackling sound if squeezed. Speech may have a nasal quality and airway obstruction may develop.

Pneumothorax. Chest pain and shortness of breath usually occur. In more severe cases the diver may develop blue skin and lose consciousness.

Air Embolism. Unconsciousness soon after surfacing, or the victim may cough up frothy fluid. A conscious victim may complain of chest pain or of localized weakness, and speech difficulties or poor balance may precede loss of consciousness.

The popularity of scuba diving has changed some impressions about air embolism. In submarine escape training most cases of embolism caused loss of consciousness soon after surfacing. In a series of thirteen cases of scuba embolism four became unconscious. Perhaps this is related to ascent rates. It is unwise to think that a scuba diver has not embolized just because he is not unconscious.

Lung Rupture

Lung rupture is not common but it is still a concern. In California's Monterey Bay area, thirteen cases of air embolism have been treated in a five year period. Each year 50,000 to 70,000 divers visit the area, so the rate of embolism is low. However, the catastrophic nature of lung rupture makes each case significant. The University of Rhode Island study concludes that about twenty diving fatalities each year result from embolism.

Proper treatment of lung rupture is difficult in most diving situations. Generally a chamber is not readily available. The victim may deteriorate so rapidly there isn't time for transportation. In serious cases even the finest care may be ineffective. Therefore, prevention must be emphasized.

Prevention starts with proper selection of diving students. Candidates with histories of lung disease must be carefully evaluated. Past lung injury or illness may predispose to future difficulties. Active pulmonary disease such as asthma or emphysema makes scuba diving hazardous. Chest X-rays are helpful in detecting lung abnormalities, but they do not reveal all defects.

Proper training reduces ascent barotrauma. Lung rupture usually results from three types of incidents. First, the diver panics and makes a breathholding ascent; second, he makes an emergency ascent because he is "out of air" or has a non-functioning regulator; and third, he panics while making an emergency ascent.

A scuba diver who loses control from any cause has a great chance of embolizing. Training and practice must stress the need to breathe normally during all scuba ascents. Divers will panic and act instinctively rather than thoughtfully. Only thorough and complete indoctrination can eliminate the inborn tendency to breathhold when the air supply is interrupted.

Diagnosis and Treatment

The first step in treatment of any malady is diagnosis. When faced with an injured diver first consider the likely possibilities. Mediastinal and subcutaneous emphysema do not usually require immediate first aid. *But any victim should be taken to a physician since serious problems may later develop.* A careful physical examination may reveal coexistent pneumothorax or even air embolism.

Unfortunately there is little a layman can do for a pneumothorax. All cases of suspected injury should be seen by a physician. A chest tube may be required but placing one should not be done without special training. Oxygen may aid respiratory distress.

Recompression therapy is not used in emphysema or in pneumothorax. It can be very dangerous in pneumothorax unless a chest tube has been placed.

Proper treatment of air embolism is immediate recompression, preferably to 165 feet. Any delay decreases the chances of survival. Do not attempt water decompression. Any unconscious scuba diver must be considered to have air embolism until proven otherwise. First aid includes:

a. Immediate transportation to a recompression facility is necessary. Have someone notify the facility of the accident so everything will be ready.

b. The victim may need cardiopulmonary resuscitation.

c. Oxygen should be administered.

d. Intravenous fluids can be helpful if someone is available to give them.

e. The head down, feet up position will direct any new bubbles away from the head. This position does not affect the bubbles that have already lodged in the brain. The head down position increases the risk of bubbles entering the coronary circulation. Tilting the victim onto his left side may reduce new bubble transport, but overdoing the head down position can make breathing difficult.

9

Emergency Ascents

Nothing is more alarming to the scuba diver than being out of air underwater. The diver's body depends on a continuous supply of air and its absence quickly arouses conscious and automatic reactions. The most basic instinct cries for an immediate return to the surface. If the diver's mind succumbs to this desire, he may fail to evaluate the situation properly and may make an unnecessary or improper emergency ascent.

Proper ascent technique is one of the most controversial subjects in diving education. The subject deserves discussion, but only after considering what makes emergency ascent necessary. This chapter will discuss the diver's management of his *own* problems.

The first step in ascent training is teaching how to recognize the need for an emergency ascent. Though simple in concept, this goal cannot be reached without effort by instructor and student. Most of the situations causing underwater distress can be managed without making an abnormal ascent. Only training and experience enable the distressed diver to react properly. For instance, pool work should teach the student that he can complete a dive without a mask.

Avoiding the Need for Emergency Ascents

There are several reasons for running out of air, but they can be reduced to a basic failure to match air supply to the requirements of the dive. Common causes of running out of air include using a partially filled tank, filling the tank with the reserve "J" valve in the "up" position, depressing the "J" valve unknowingly during the dive, using more air than expected, or ignoring a submersible pressure gauge.

Being truly "out of air" is unusual since a scuba tank is never really drained of air, even when the gauge reads zero. On ascent the residual tank air expands and can be breathed. This can be safely verified in a little experiment. Using a tank with a functioning "J" valve, dive to 30-50 feet and stay until difficult inhalation signals depletion of your air supply. Without pulling the "J" valve, begin to calmly swim upward while breathing normally. Do not hold your breath. As you ascend, you will find that inhalation again becomes easy. If you overbreathe this "new" air supply, you can just pull your "J" valve, but with calm breathing, you will not need to use the reserve.

The use of submersible pressure gauges should virtually eliminate the surprise "out of air" situation. Of course, the gauge must be used to be of value. Planning to surface well before reaching zero on the gauge insures adequate ascent air in the tank. Diving in closed spaces like caves or wrecks makes air supply monitoring especially crucial since immediate ascent may be impossible.

A non-functional or lost regulator naturally renders even a full tank useless. A regulator can be briefly misplaced, but is rarely lost except in a serious entanglement. Modern regulators rarely fail unless very poorly maintained. There are plenty of anecdotes about regulator failure accidents, but research has not identified fatalities caused by properly maintained regulators.

In brief, a true "out of air" situation is rare in scuba. This means that most ascents can be made normally, even if the situation prompting the ascent is unusual such as the cold or a cut foot. Because rare instances of sudden, unexpected air supply termination do occur, every scuba diver must be prepared to deal with the problem.

Meeting the Challenge

No emergency ascent technique is perfect; each has its advantages and disadvantages. The thoughtful instructor discusses the various methods and makes suggestions. The diver should formulate emergency plans before beginning a dive. Few people think calmly when frightened and this is not the time for prolonged evaluation of possible responses.

The basic steps in accident management begin when the diver recognizes that an emergency exists. Once he does that, he must decide on a course of action, then carry out that action.

When it comes to recognizing an "out of air" situation most divers will overreact rather than fail to note the problem. Evaluate the problem by asking some questions: Is the situation truly an emergency? Is the regulator in your mouth? Were you just breathing too fast? Is the "J" valve pulled?

These checks can be made by all but the most emotionally upset diver. Once an air termination is confirmed virtually every diver gets scared. A decision must be made and time is important. There is not time to pull out a manual and study ascent techniques.

The typical diver heads for the surface without signalling to his buddy. Unfortunately, he often instinctively holds his breath. The well trained diver recognizes the problem and calmly begins a proper emergency ascent.

Independent Ascents

The solo diver, or the diver whose buddy has strayed, must make an independent ascent. He depends on his own wits and equipment. Every diver needs to learn independent ascent techniques. They are simpler than the dependent techniques and do not require another person.

There are three basic types of independent emergency ascents: free ascents, swimming ascents, and buoyant ascents.

The *free ascent* is made without any propulsive effort. Air that expands on *ascent* is continuously exhaled with the rate of exhalation balanced against the rate of ascent through the water. Speed of ascent should be just less than that of the bubbles as they rise. When the diver begins to pass through his bubbles, he increases exhalation and slows ascent. When he falls behind his bubbles, he slows exhalation and ascent rate will increase. This technique works. However, it is very difficult and has been the most dangerous of submarine escape training methods. It is *not* recommended for scuba divers.

The *swimming ascent* is the most reliable and least dangerous technique for scuba ascent from shallow to moderate depths. The diver swims to the surface and exhales as he goes. Unless the regulator is hopelessly broken, it should be kept in the mouth since some inhalation can be made. It is obviously important to exhale throughout the ascent. This technique provides a reliable upward propulsive force while being slow enough to provide venting of the expanding lungs.

It is possible to exhale too much during a free ascent and run out of air and upward momentum. It is difficult to run out of air while making a swimming ascent. A diver can run out of air if he tries very hard and swims very slowly. But with normal exhalation force and reasonable speed, there will be plenty of air.

During a dive an average sized diver has about four liters of air in his lungs after exhalation. As he ascends, this air volume expands in accordance with Boyle's Law. Four liters of air at thirty-three feet would become eight liters at the surface. Thus, the ascending diver can blow off four liters and still have plenty of air in his lungs.

Buoyant ascents provide a more rapid and effortless ride to the surface. With standard scuba equipment, it is difficult to predict how fast ascent will be. This depends on depth, size of vest, how much gas is put in the vest, the diver's preinflation buoyancy, and posture during ascent.

Submarine escapes are made at over 300 feet per minute. This doesn't provide much time for exhalation. The usual scuba vest wouldn't provide this much lift but speed remains the most important drawback to buoyant ascent. Besides the problem of exhaling, there is the problem of rapidly ascending into something, like the hull of a boat. Buoyant ascent can be helpful from deep depths where swimming becomes tiring. The vest, of course, expands during ascent and makes ascent accelerative. This can be dangerous as lung volume changes most rapidly near the surface.

One way to increase buoyancy and make swimming easier is to ditch the weight belt. Unless the diver uses enormous amounts of weight, this will not drastically speed up ascent. Remember that as the surface is neared the wet suit will reexpand and increase buoyancy. Again, this occurs at the same time that lung volume is increasing most rapidly.

Dependent Ascents

Competent buddies can make dependent ascents with one diver providing air for the other. Dependent ascents have been successful and unsuccessful. When they go wrong, unfortunately, it is not uncommon for both divers to die.

As with independent ascents, there are a variety of techniques. All depend on a smoothly functioning buddy team. This means that the divers have discussed and practiced cooperative breathing. The buddies must stay in contact and have a way to signal in case of emergency. The dependent ascent techniques probably will not work with buddies who do not frequently dive together. Both divers must be very competent and trusting.

Dependent ascents violate a basic principle of lifesaving: stay out of the victim's grasp. When a diver loses his air he can quickly become dangerously irrational. He may grab his buddy's regulator without warning. If given a regulator to share, he may refuse to give it back. This is scary business and the risk must not be ignored. In your effort to help your buddy do not ignore your own safety.

The oldest method of dependent ascent is *buddy breathing*. The diver with air takes a breath and then passes his regulator to the victim for a breath. This can be done face to face or over the back. Face to face has the advantage of facial contact which is often reassuring. The technique can be and should be practiced in a swimming pool.

It works well under two conditions. Both divers must cooperate, and one of the buddies must have an adequate air supply. Cooperation, of course, is essential. Neither can hog the regulator. Often both divers run out of air at almost the same time. Then buddy breathing fails.

The octopus rig is a second regulator attached to the first stage of the primary regulator. When both buddies use an octopus, there is no need to share regulators for dependent ascents. This provides a very real advantage over buddy breathing as no one has to be without a regulator. Recently, some educators have said that octopus rigs have made buddy breathing obsolete. This is not yet true.

The octopus has not solved all ascent problems. The divers still must communicate and work together. Some regulators don't work well in tandem when tank pressure is low. It still places a diver at risk from an irrational victim. And if both divers run out of air, the octopus can't help. There have been fatalities involving buddy pairs who were wearing functional octopi. The octopus is easier to use than buddy breathing, but still requires practice.

Some divers use a secondary or pony tank with a regulator for emergency air. These are especially popular with cave and wreck divers. They make independent ascents or dependent ascents easier. When used in the dependent mode, the problem of cooperation and sharing remains. Pony bottles definitely make a contribution to safer diving. Most divers don't find that their potential value justifies their cost or the inconvenience of carrying still more equipment.

Teaching Emergency Ascents

Every diving training organization recognizes that emergency ascent training is important. There is still no uniform agreement on how this training should be accomplished. Two basic problems make ascent training a difficult subject. First, ascent training is risky, and secondly, ascent training often doesn't simulate reality. Many diving skills are difficult, few are dangerous. Emergency ascents are both difficult and dangerous. Every abnormal ascent introduces the possibility of lung rupture and air embolism.

Actual ascent training must involve ascending. Taking a breath and exhaling during a swim along the bottom of a pool does not realistically simulate what happens during an ascent. The sensation of exhaling expanding air can only occur during an ascent. But making even an ascent from ten feet can be hazardous.

The dependent ascent techniques can be taught more easily than independent ones. Both buddy breathing and use of the octopus can be taught in the pool. Ascents with the octopus can be safely supervised, since breathing is completely normal. Buddy breathing ascents are more hazardous, since there may be short phases of ascending without the usual inhalation/exhalation cycle. Supervision in open water can be difficult. When the regulator is surrendered, the diver must not hold his breath while ascending.

There are not many instructors sufficiently trained to teach emergency ascent techniques. So many misconceptions abound. One is that ascents require complete exhaling down to residual volume before beginning. This is a misinterpretation of the Navy's term "blow and go" which actually means to start blowing and then go while continuing to exhale. A continuous rather than forceful exhalation is required. Another misconception frequently passed on to students is that they are likely to run out of air. This is highly unlikely except in a free ascent or very slow swimming ascent. Unless the diver is very slow, he will have plenty of oxygen for the ascent.

The biggest misconception is that there is a safe way to practice independent emergency ascents. With a careful selection of candidates and very thorough supervision, the risk of accidents can be reduced. It cannot be completely eliminated. From one third to one half of all air embolisms occur during ascent training. Many instructors have taught emergency ascents without accidents. A smaller group has had accidents in training, and they are not likely to forget them. The penalty for a failed ascent is very stiff.

The Submarine Escape Training Tower at Pearl Harbor

Divers and instructors who support ascent training have sound arguments. Divers need to know how to get out of trouble and this is inadequately learned by lectures and unrealistic drills. A diver who has made a simulated emergency ascent may be more confident and secure in future dives. Most people can practice ascents without embolizing if conditions are ideal.

Arguments can also be made against ascent training. Accidents cannot be completely avoided during ascent training. Too much emphasis is placed on emergency ascent rather than on diving so that it is unlikely to have an "out of air" situation. The incidence of "out of air" situations is too low to justify the risk of ascent training. Practice sessions usually cannot be realistic enough to prepare a diver for a true emergency. The benefits of ascent training must be weighed against the risks.

10

The Diver and Temperatures

A Hawaiian diver came to California for a vacation. His first abalone dive began shockingly as ice cold water covered his head and poured into his rented wet suit. A laughing buddy suggested that he put the suit hood over his head rather than let it dangle behind him. The Hawaiian was also surprised at how hard it was to use his hands in the water. On the next dive, he wore gloves.

A diver will chill in water the same temperature as comfortable air temperature. Water conducts heat twenty-five times better than air and has a 1,000 times greater specific heat. Heat always runs downhill and the high specific heat means much more heat is required to warm the water. Water of 33 degrees Centigrade to 35 degrees Centigrade would be required to avoid heat loss.

Cold initially is uncomfortable. Then it inhibits function and at extreme limits can be deadly. Cold is one of the major limitations to dive duration for recreational and commercial divers.

The scuba diver also loses heat through having to heat and moisten the air he breathes from a cold tank. This effect worsens as dive depth increases the gas density. Respiratory heat loss may be 25 percent of total heat loss.

The human body functions properly only within a narrow temperature range. If the central (core) temperature changes one degree Centigrade in either direction, discomfort is obvious. A three degree rise or four degree fall in the core will often be fatal. Fortunately several mechanisms keep temperatures normal despite environmental challenges.

Upon immersion skin temperature quickly falls. In 24 degree C water (warmer than most oceans) skin temperature falls about eight degrees in one hour, most of this in thirty minutes. Central temperature only decreases by about one-third of a degree in an hour. Central heat loss is reduced by the layer of subcutaneous fat which insulates the body, increased heat production, reduction in blood flow to the skin and extremities, and counter current heat exchange.

Fat is a much better insulator than lean tissue. The fat layer reduces direct heat transfer from the central body to the skin and water. Total immersion times are greater in fat persons than in lean ones. Women have proportionately more subcutaneous fat for a given weight which provides them an advantage in cold water.

Oxygen consumption and heat production rise in water immersion. This will match heat loss to a certain point. When body temperature falls, shivering further raises heat production.

Skin cools quickly because of its water contact, but also because of the constriction of blood vessels which keep warm blood from it. Functionally, the outer parts of the body are sacrificed to maintain core temperature. Blood flow to the scalp does not change. Therefore, the head loses a great deal of heat; about 50 percent of body heat exits through the head. Shivering is one but not the only reason that skin vasoconstriction is interrupted by periods of vasodilation. Shivering increases heat production but also increases blood flow to the extremities which may cause a net increase in heat loss.

Warm blood flowing out from the core warms returning venous blood. Counter current heat exchange thus sends cold blood to the periphery of the body while warming that blood which returns to the central organs.

Effects of Cold

Both physical and mental changes result from water exposure The fingers lose their sensitivity and the hands become weak and clumsy. These changes worsen with time and degree of cold. Performance of tasks requiring mental function fails in a somewhat different way. With time, cold itself reduces mental acuity. But before this, mental function is impaired by a "distraction" effect of cold water. The diver becomes aware of being cold and this takes his attention away from other matters. The distraction happens almost immediately upon entering the water and is present even before central body temperature changes.

With continued cooling the swimmer develops lethargy and becomes confused. The effort of remaining functional while cold is fatiguing. These effects act together to increase the possibility of anxiety and panic.

Tolerance to Cold

There are no firm definitions of tolerable cold exposure. In general, a cold exposure is related to both temperature and duration of exposure. Cold tolerance depends on mental status, physical state, clothing worn, activity in the water, and adaptation to cold.

Beyond a certain point, cold will affect all persons almost equally. But in the ranges experienced by most scuba divers there is wide variation depending on mental states. Dedicated divers can work when others fail. Unfortunately, the diver who can "stand" cold water may actually be at great risk since he may voluntarily stay beyond the time where physical impairment begins. This diver may lose physical capabilities and be injured while his less hardy friends were saved by leaving the water earlier.

Physical state includes body build. As discussed earlier, a fat layer improves cold tolerance. Of course, true obesity has many disadvantages in diving.

Clothing provides an artificial layer of insulation and inhibits heat loss. Diving suits for commercial diving have become very efficient. Recreational suits are less effective as will be discussed later.

Activity in the water increases heat production. It also increases blood flow which augments heat loss to the water. The net result depends on water temperature and degree of exertion. In very cold water (0-5 degrees C) exertion is dangerous. However, at temperatures above 24 degrees C, activity reduces net heat loss. As the activity becomes more vigorous, the tolerable water temperature falls. But, of course, exercise eventually causes fatigue.

Studies of the ama (a group of women divers from Korea and Japan) and of polar divers suggest that physical adaptation to cold water does exist. This is separate from the mental adaptation which gives a motivated diver an edge over a novice. Physiological changes may improve cold tolerance after prolonged exposures. But the average scuba diver making a few weekend dives will not become physically adapted to cold.

Improving Tolerance

Diving suits have made diving more enjoyable and safer. Most recreational divers use neoprene wet or dry suits. The rubber, with its trapped air cells, provides added insulation. In the wet suit a thin layer of water is quickly warmed to provide another insulating layer. The insulation retains heat produced by the exercising diver. This type of suit (wet or dry) has definite limitations, including the fact that insulation is limited by mobility and buoyancy; insulation is not feasible for all of the body; and pressure will decrease the suit's protective value.

A suit that will protect the diver in very cold water would have to be over one-half inch thick. This limits movement and makes the suit very buoyant. An excessive amount of weight would be necessary to make submergence possible. Thin suits work well only when the diver is swimming hard and do not function too well if the diver is at rest. The fingers lose heat quickly since they have large surface area. Complete insulation of them is not practical and some functional impairment must be accepted. Mittens retain heat better than gloves.

Descent shrinks the air cells within the neoprene thus decreasing buoyancy and insulation. At 150 feet a typical wet suit has one quarter of its surface insulating capacity. Deep water, of course, tends to be colder than the surface. The air space inside a dry suit also decreases with depth unless a constant volume suit is used.

Suits do not prevent heat loss, but they do slow the loss. In an experiment with a 3/10-inch suit, body core temperature fell in two hours the same as in one hour without a suit.

Suit effectiveness can be improved by noting that:

a. Thickness improves insulation. Several layers work better than a single thick layer.

b. The head and chest are the two most important areas.

c. Zippers decrease insulation.

d. Unlined rubber insulates better and prevents continual influx of cold water from movement in the water.

Diving techniques also affect temperature tolerance. Being rested and nourished before the dive starts your body at a good metabolic point and provides fuel for heat production. If you start a dive fatigued and hungry you impair your compensatory responses to cold.

Start your dive warm, as physical tolerance for a given dive depends on skin and core temperature. If you start diving while cold, it takes less time to reach your cold threshold. Do not stand around in a bathing suit before the dive.

More importantly, do not stand around half naked *after* the dive. When the immersion ends blood flow returns to normal and cold peripheral blood enters the central body. Typically, core temperature continues to fall after the cold exposure ends. If you intend to make a second dive, be sure you have rewarmed from the first dive. After an hour in cold water it takes at least an hour in a warm environment to recover the lost heat.

The best method of rewarming is to take a long, hot bath. A shower is not as good because the skin warms at the expense of the central body. A sudden shift of blood to the periphery may cause fainting. Drinking warm liquids may make you feel good but will not do much for rewarming. Alcohol, again, is dangerous because it increases skin heat loss and dulls the brain.

The diver will feel warm and comfortable before total rewarming of the inner core has taken place, so comfort cannot be used as the sole judge of recovery.

Preventing Cold Injury

The average recreational diver will not have serious cold problems unless he tries to be heroic. Following the guidelines presented will maximize cold tolerance. When the water becomes uncomfortable, stop the dive. Do not try to push to the point of actual shivering. Wet suited, active swimmers will not shiver until their core temperatures have dropped more than a degree. Functional deficiencies appear at this temperature and the typical additional temperature reduction after ending the dive can be dangerous. You don't need a water or body thermometer to know when to quit. Stop when the fun stops.

Be certain not to reenter the water until you are completely warm. This determination is difficult because adequate rewarming is not well related to body temperature, comfort, or cessation of shivering. Remember, it may take an hour in a bath. If you cannot have a warm bath, it will take longer. Deaths have occurred from repeated diving after heat loss.

Profound Cold Exposure

Very few scuba divers choose to dive in waters of 0-5 degrees C. Those who do, need special exposure suits and must be very careful. The results of exposure to frigid waters are somewhat different than temperate water exposure. A lightly clothed person can survive only about fifteen minutes at zero degrees C and about an hour at 5 degrees C.

Activity in very cold water decreases survival time. Swimming becomes virtually impossible as the severe cold causes hyperventilation and then respiratory distress. In one study at 4.7 degrees C, no one was able to swim 275 yards and maximum voluntary tolerance was less than twelve minutes. The lean swimmers were incapacitated before their body temperature changed. Life vests are especially important during boat trips in frigid waters.

Severe body chilling makes the heart susceptible to serious rhythm disturbances. A victim of profound cold exposure must be handled very gently and moved only as necessary. Movement may cause the heart to fibrillate, resulting in death. Prompt rewarming in a bath is essential. These victims may have impaired breathing and heart action, and should be evaluated by a physician as soon as possible.

Overheating

In commercial diving, which utilizes pressure chambers, overheating has been a problem and has caused fatalities. The recreational diver, however, may overheat while on land (or ship) before a dive. Overheating results from increased body heat production, gaining heat from the environment, and reduced ability to eliminate body heat.

A diver who makes a long hike to a dive site, carrying his gear, increases body heat through exercise. A hot day will intensify this heat again. Normally, people efficiently cool off by sweating. In humid climates this becomes ineffective. A diver, wearing a wet suit while hiking, severely restricts body heat loss.

Heat illness progresses through three phases: first, heat cramps, then heat exhaustion (heat prostration), and finally heat stroke (sunstroke). Heat cramps occur through the loss of salt and other electrolytes. Body temperature is normal. Heat cramps are the most common heat injury in diving and can be prevented by using extra salt with meals in hot weather or when very active.

Heat exhaustion results from deficiencies in both salt and fluids. Fatigue and headache accompany muscle cramping. Body temperature is usually normal, but may be low or slightly elevated. During exertion an effort must be made to drink heavily. People exposed to heat stress may voluntarily fail to drink enough.

With heat stroke, body temperature rises rapidly. Heat elimination fails and sweating will cease. Healthy people rarely get heat stroke without extremely vigorous exercise while dehydrated on hot, humid days. With markedly elevated body temperatures every system of the body fails. Confusion and convulsions precede liver, kidney, heart, muscle, and coagulation failure. Heat stroke has a very high mortality rate and requires immediate, aggressive therapy beginning with body cooling.

Divers rarely exercise enough to get heat stroke. But their use of wet suits and their tendency toward inadequate fluid intake make heat cramps and exhaustion quite possible. On long hikes it would be better to carry, rather than wear, the wet suit. Heavy fluid intake before and after dives is important. Use plenty of salt with meals, but avoid salt tablets as they are very rarely necessary and can cause excessive body salt levels. At the first sign of cramps or fatigue stop exercising and cool down. No sensible diver need be among the 4,000 people in the U.S. who die of heat injury each year.

11

Decompression Sickness

Not long ago the skipper of a southern California diving boat complained about the growing emphasis on diving safety.

"These instructors and their scare stories are ruining my business," he said. "Who cares about things that never happen? I've been diving ten years and I don't need any of those tables. Just stop at ten feet for a few minutes and you're all right."

Recently this man made two quick dives to 150 feet and, despite past experience, found how real decompression sickness can be. After extensive physical therapy, he can walk again, with the help of leg braces.

The multifaceted malady of decompression sickness results from pressure effects on gases carried throughout the circulatory system from the lungs to the tissues. During a dive using compressed air, nitrogen pressure throughout the body rises toward ambient nitrogen pressure. The elevated pressures cause nitrogen accumulation in all the tissues. Upon ascent, nitrogen pressure falls and the excess tissue nitrogen enters the blood for exhalation from the lungs. If the ascent rate exceeds safe value, nitrogen will form bubbles throughout the body. (Nitrogen accumulation and decompression sickness can also result from closely spaced, deep breath-hold dives but this is uncommon.)

Bubble formation is a complex subject. The tendency to bubbling basically depends on the amount of nitrogen present and the speed at which pressure decreases. Nitrogen accumulation depends on time and depth of exposure. It takes more than twenty-four hours to completely saturate the body with nitrogen. Nitrogen uptake proceeds exponentially until saturation. A long dive increases the risk of decompression sickness. Similarly, the deeper a dive the more nitrogen will be taken up for a given dive duration.

The accumulated excess nitrogen causes no problems until ascent when ambient pressure begins to decrease. A slow ascent permits orderly transfer of the nitrogen from tissue to blood to lungs. Too rapid an ascent overwhelms the transfer system. Safe ascent rate depends on the amount of nitrogen present. Long, deep dives require slower ascents.

The tendency to bubble formation varies among the tissues. Thus, an ascent rate that might be safe for the liver would be too fast for the knee. Bubbles can form in any tissue. They most often form in low pressure areas such as veins and capillaries and in areas of high nitrogen solubility and poor vascularity such as fat and joints. Bubbles sometimes form within the cells.

Once formed, bubbles expand on ascent. They cause decompression sickness by mechanically obstructing blood flow and by direct pressure on tissues. Bubbles also act indirectly by reacting with components of blood. Activity at the bubble surface causes clumping of red blood cells and platelets. The blood coagulation mechanism may be inappropriately activated. All these processes cause sluggish blood flow that adds to obstruction from the bubbles themselves. Plasma volume falls in decompression sickness and this further impedes blood flow.

Decompression sickness affects several body systems including the skin, joints, central nervous system (brain and spinal cord), peripheral nervous system, lungs, and the bones.

Decompression sickness is often divided into two types. Type one includes skin and joint problems, and type two includes more serious disorders. Symptoms of decompression sickness usually appear within an hour of surfacing but may not appear for twenty-four hours. The onset may be catastrophic, but usually in recreational diving, the symptoms develop more gradually than in cerebral air embolism. Chapter 13 discusses the need to suspect decompression sickness when illness follows a scuba dive. Minor symptoms may be antecedents of severe involvement. Decompression sickness rarely kills, but it can cripple and therefore deserves respect.

Most decompression sickness causes joint pain in one of several areas. Most divers have more arm than leg involvement. The term "bends" refers to this musculoskeletal form of decompression sickness. Usually, bends is not accompanied by swelling, discoloration, warmth, or tenderness of the joint. This helps distinguish it from injuries or infections.

Skin decompression may cause a rash but more often is manifested by itching. Sport divers have fewer skin problems than deep divers.

Aviators get brain decompression sickness, but it is less common in diving. Involvement of the spinal cord, unfortunately, is common in diving decompression sickness. Spinal cord damage disrupts sensory function, muscle function, and autonomic function (bowel and bladder). Peripheral nerve involvement causes localized areas of weakness, numbness, or abnormal sensation. Severe decompression sickness may affect the inner ear.

Venous bubbles may go to the lungs, and in sufficient numbers, will impair pulmonary circulation. The resultant "chokes" take longer to develop and is unusual in scuba diving. "Chokes" causes respiratory discomfort and impaired function.

Bone damage does not occur soon after surfacing. It takes time —months or years—and is often found only on skeletal X-rays. Areas of dead bone, aseptic necrosis, may be found in divers who have never had obvious symptoms of decompression sickness. Generally, aseptic bone necrosis is thought to result from frequent, marginally unsafe commercial diving. But research is slim in this area, and reports indicate that sport divers are also subject to bone necrosis.

PREVENTING DECOMPRESSION SICKNESS

Prevention of decompression sickness depends on limiting the amount of nitrogen absorbed and by providing adequate time for orderly nitrogen elimination. In the early 1900s, J.S. Haldane proposed that the body could stand a certain degree of over-pressurization without bubble formation. A rough approximation of Haldane's theories is that the body can stand a rapid twofold reduction in pressure. Thus, ascent from a dive of thirty-three feet (two atmosphere absolute) to the surface (one atmosphere) should be safe. The theory has been modified in several ways since tissues vary in their gas tolerance. Experience has proven the subject more complex than originally realized. Complete gas elimination takes much longer than expected.

The development of the ultrasonic bubble detector, which uses the Doppler principle, has drastically revised theories of decompression.* Not infrequently, bubbles can be heard after dives

---

*The Doppler principle involves the theory that the pitch of the sound made by a moving object increases as the object approaches the listener, then diminishes as it passes away. Bubble detectors can "hear" the change in noise as an air bubble passes through the blood.

which are not accompanied by any evidence of decompression sickness. Apparently, standard decompression does not prevent bubbling; rather it prevents symptomatic bubbles. Perhaps continued exposure to bubbles may cause chronic damage such as in bone necrosis. Interest is increasing in the development of decompression schedules that would reduce the incidence of bubbling.

Decompression tables relate dive depth and time. The tables set out requirements for safe decompression from dives. Within certain limits, ascent can be direct and this table is called the "no decompression table." The term is misleading since the ascent rate at sixty feet per minute (ft./min.) definitely allows some decompression. When dives exceed "no decompression" limits, stops are made to permit nitrogen elimination. A system to account for accumulated nitrogen from multiple dives permits use of the repetitive dive tables. (*See chapter* 12 *on decompression tables for details.*)

There are many ways to calculate decompression tables. In the United States, the U.S. Navy tables are the most widely used. The tables are not perfect, and in fact, they were not designed to be perfect. Completely eliminating the risk of decompression sickness would require very restrictive tables. A failure rate of two to three percent was accepted. Initially, the actual failure rate seemed to be about one percent. More accurate recording of number of exposures has determined the Navy's overall decompression sickness rate to be less than one half of one percent. Another analysis suggests that for air diving the incidence is closer to 0.047 percent or about five accidents in every 10,000 dives.

The risk of decompression sickness is not great. However, it increases with improper diving and can be affected by personal factors. Most frequently, decompression sickness results from ignoring the decompression tables, using the wrong tables, or improperly measuring dive depth or duration. Even proper diving, however, can end with decompression sickness.

People vary widely in their susceptibility to decompression sickness. Ultrasonic bubble detection has shown that propensity to bubbling varies among individuals, and from day to day for any given diver.

Several factors seem to affect susceptibility to decompression sickness. They include the diver's age, body build, activity during dive and decompression, water temperature, carbon dioxide accumulation, alcohol useage, and adaptation to pressure.

Age is one of the most reliable influences on susceptibility. Older divers have a higher incidence of decompression sickness. With aging, the circulatory system generally loses some of its efficiency. This may impair nitrogen elimination and cause bubbling. Uptake of nitrogen may also be slower but since ascent is usually shorter than bottom time, the problem is with gas elimination.

Obesity also increases decompression sickness. Fat holds more nitrogen and overweight people have impaired circulation. On short dives, the fat storage of nitrogen is less of a problem since fat takes up nitrogen relatively slowly.

Exercise increases gas uptake and elimination. In theory, exercising during decompression should help prevent decompression sickness by improving nitrogen elimination. In fact, however, exercise during decompression *increases* decompression sickness. Evidently, bubbling is made more likely by muscle activity.

Carbon dioxide accumulation intensifies bubble formation. This will not be a problem in scuba diving except with excessive skip breathing.

Drinking alcohol before a dive, which has already been discussed, appears to increase the rate of decompression sickness. Cold water diving may also increase decompression sickness. These are observations whose mechanisms have not been established.

Commercial divers appear to have a lower decompression sickness incidence after prolonged diving. This may be true adaptation since interrupting the diving will increase susceptibility. Recreational divers do not usually dive consistently enough to develop tolerance.

Because decompression sickness restricts diving, there is continued interest in discovering a medicine to prevent it. The search continues, although nothing has been found to be very effective. Current research centers around drugs to reduce blood clumping but even the prevention of clumping would not solve the initial insult—bubble formation.

Treatment

All scuba divers need to be familiar with principles of decompression sickness management. Unfortunately, many accidents are poorly managed and result in permanent disability to the victim. Details of management are found in chapter 13. The initial principle is to consider the possibility of decompression sickness in an injured divers. Failure to recognize the possibility worsens the problem.

Definitve therapy of all cases, except skin decompression sickness, requires recompression and then gradual decompression. Most facilities now use the low pressure oxygen treatment tables which give better results in less time than the old air tables. Recompression to sixty feet is followed by alternating oxygen and air breathing (to reduce the risk of oxygen toxicity) with subsequent decompression to thirty feet where the oxygen/air cycles continue. Finally, slow decompression is made to the surface with the victim breathing oxygen. The new tables take a maximum of six hours while the old tables took more than thirty hours. Repeated recompression treatment may be necessary.

Supplementary therapy may involve giving intravenous fluids, steroids, and respiratory, and cardiovascular support.

Success of therapy depends on the seriousness of the accident, the promptness of treatment, and the use of the correct treatment programs. It is very important to treat without undue delay. Response can be seen in late therapy, but it is often less satisfactory. Damage from bubble formation, swelling of the spinal cord for example, may not respond well to recompression.

12

Using Decompression Tables

"Now, let's see. If I make a dive to 120 feet for twenty minutes, is that the same as twenty feet for 120 minutes?"

"You say make the deep dive first, but I left my depth gauge at home."

"I've got a new table here that looks pretty simple. It came in a cereal box."

"Let's leave the instructor to deal with these students and try to solve the mystery of decompression tables."

All scuba divers need to be familiar with standard Navy decompression tables. These tables are computed to coordinate dive depth and duration so that surfacing will not cause decompression sickness. The tables permit ascent when the amount of dissolved gas is within safe limits.

The Navy tables have been validated through wide useage. Because of their safety record, they are recommended for recreational use in preference to any unofficial tables. As will be discussed, Navy tables apply better to hard hat diving than to scuba diving, but there is no adequate substitute.

No safety factors are added to decompression times in the tables. Failures are expected since elimination of failures would make the tables very restrictive. The tables do not always eliminate nitrogen bubble formation, but they usually prevent symptoms from these bubbles. Individual variations, such as obesity or advanced age, may result in decompression sickness despite adherence to standard procedures. Ignoring decompression principles markedly increases the risk of decompression sickness.

The Navy has decompression tables for several types of diving. Recreational divers need only use the standard air tables, the "no decompression" table, and the repetitive dive tables. Familiarity with a table does not mean memorizing it. The tables should be taken on dive trips and be used to plan the diving day. Use them to check on procedures and to make suitable adjustments when the actual dive varies from the plan.

The standard air table actually exceeds recreational divers' needs since it accounts for dives as deep as 190 feet and for decompression time of almost three hours. A derivative of this table officially named "no decompression limit and repetitive group designation table for no-decompression air dives" is the scuba diver's friend. It defines the time/depth constraints which permit direct surfacing without need for decompression stops.

Avoid dives that require decompression stops. The "no decompression" table is easy to learn and mistakes are, therefore, less common. Failure rates are much lower for dives that do not require decompression stops. In scuba diving there are several problems in making decompression dives. These include:

a. adequate air supply for the stops

b. control of stop depth

c. proper timing of stop duration

d. cold and fatigue during stops

e. communication

f. seasickness

The "no decompression" table is not overly restrictive for recreational diving. The inclusion of limits for dives below 120 feet should not suggest you dive that deep. Usually, air supply proves more limiting than the table.

Certain principles apply for all dives:

a. Bottom time is the time from leaving the surface to the beginning of the ascent.

b. Dive depth is the maximum depth reached at any time during the dive.

c. Descent rate is not important as it is part of bottom time.

d. Ascent should be at 60 feet per minute. Going faster reduces the time for nitrogen elimination. Going slower permits continued gas uptake by some slow tissues.

e. When either time or depth is between two groups, the next larger or deeper should be used.

f. Do not modify the tables. Safety can be increased by being conservative in choice of depth and time. For instance, stay only 30 minutes on an 80 foot dive.

TABLE I
NO-DECOMPRESSION LIMITS AND REPETITIVE GROUP DESIGNATION TABLE FOR NO-DECOMPRESSION AIR DIVES

Depth (feet)	No-decompression limits (min)	A	B	C	D	E	F	G	H	I	J	K	L	M	N	O
10		60	120	210	300											
15		35	70	110	160	225	350									
20		25	50	75	100	135	180	240	325							
25		20	35	55	75	100	125	160	195	245	315					
30		15	30	45	60	75	95	120	145	170	205	250	310			
35	310	5	15	25	40	50	60	80	100	120	140	160	190	220	270	310
40	200	5	15	25	30	40	50	70	80	100	110	130	150	170	200	
50	100		10	15	25	30	40	50	60	70	80	90	100			
60	60		10	15	20	25	30	40	50	55	60					
70	50		5	10	15	20	30	35	40	45	50					
80	40		5	10	15	20	25	30	35	40						
90	30		5	7	12	15	20	25	30							
100	25			5	10	15	20	25								
110	20			5	10	13	15	20								
120	15			5	10	12	15									
130	10			5	8	10										
140	10			5	7	10										
150	5			5												
160	5				5											
170	5				5											
180	5				5											
190	5				5											

Group Designation

THE REPETITIVE DIVE SYSTEM

The nitrogen accumulated during a dive decreases rapidly, but some of it will remain in the body for at least 24 hours. If one dive is followed by another, the final amount of absorbed nitrogen is the sum of that remaining from the first dive plus that taken up on the second dive. It would be dangerous to ignore the first dive in computing decompression requirements for the second one. The simplest way to schedule a second dive is to treat both dives as one to the deeper depth and then add bottom times.

Example: A diver goes to 80 feet for 30 minutes. Then he wants to make a second dive to 50 feet. He could safely consider this combination as a single dive to 80 feet and would then be able to stay 10 minutes on the 50 foot excursion.

REPETITIVE DIVE WORKSHEET

First Dive

depth _80 ft._   **repetitive group** _G_

bottom time _30 min_   from "no decompression" table

Surface interval

_2_ hours _0_ minutes   (use residual nitrogen timetable)

beginning group _G_

new group _D_

Second dive   (from residual nitrogen timetable)

depth _50 ft._

residual nitrogen time _29 min._

bottom time _11 min._   **new repetitive group** _L_

total time _100 min._   from "no decompression" table

Surface Interval   repeat as above

Third Dive

Another way to arrange repeated dives is the infamous repetitive dive system. During the interval between dives, nitrogen leaves the body. When the second dive begins, the amount of excess nitrogen is less than upon surfacing from the first dive. The gas leaves exponentially during the surface interval; fast at first and then more slowly. The Navy has calculated elimination rates and incorporates them into the residual nitrogen timetable. Credit is given for nitrogen eliminated and a penalty assigned for that which remains.

Admittedly the repetitive dive system is a wee bit complicated, but it does make repetitive diving more practical. Recreation divers need to know how to work the repetitive dive tables. That is, of course, unless they prefer adding bottom times, or they never want to dive more than once a day.

A repetitive dive is any dive separated from the preceding one by at least 10 minutes and by not more than 12 hours. Two dives separated by less than 10 minutes must be considered a single dive. Dives separated by 12 hours can be ignored. This is incorrect, really, since complete nitrogen elimination takes longer than 12 hours. After 12 hours, however, most of the nitrogen has been eliminated. This is especially true for short, recreational dives. In practice, the 12 hour limit has not been dangerous.

The best way to understand the system is to do some problems. With practice, you will decide the tables were not designed as a punishment for divers. The Navy's tables are reproduced here. Several systems have been designed that rearrange the tables in an effort to make them easier. These systems are fine, but it is useful to study the basic way first as it helps to understand the principles of repetitive diving.

Your efforts will be easier if you use a worksheet similar to the one presented. The tables are marked 1, 2, and 3 for convenience. To start, take the diver who goes to 80 feet for 30 minutes. The "no decompression" table (table 1) shows him in the "G" group. Assume he waits for 2 hours before diving again. Find "G" on the diagonal of the residual nitrogen time table (table 2). Move across to the column for two hours of surface survival. The time spans are presented in hours and minutes, i.e., 2:00 is two hours, 2:58 is two hours and fifty-eight minutes. Then go vertically *down* to find the next group which is D. Be careful and do not go vertically up as you will be hopelessly lost.

Our sample diver went down three groups to D because of the gas lost during the two hour surface interval. The second dive our

diver made was to fifty feet. The repetitive groups after the surface interval are listed along the top of table 3 (the second part of
the residual nitrogen timetable). Find D and go down until it
intersects with the horizontal line from the depth figures on the
left side of the table. The residual nitrogen is 29 minutes.

Almost done, but here comes the tricky part. The residual
nitrogen time can be viewed as a penalty for starting the dive with
nitrogen left over from the first dive. The total nitrogen after the
second dive is the *sum* of that from the first dive and that accumulated on the second dive. It is the same as thinking that a certain
amount of time has already been spent at the depth of the second
dive.

The whole system is designed to determine this time for any
depth of the second dive. If our diver had planned a 60 foot dive,
his penalty time would have been 24 minutes. It is less for a
deeper dive because nitrogen is taken up faster as depth increases
so that a given amount of residual nitrogen represents less time.
This is not inconsistent with safety since permissable "no decompression" limits are much less for deeper dives. In our example,
the diver wanted to stay as long as possible at 50 feet. Since the
"no decompression" limit is 100 minutes, he can make a 71 minute dive (100 minutes minus the 29 minute residual nitrogen penalty). Permissable time for a 60 foot dive would be 36 minutes.

At the end of the second dive he would be in group L and could
make a third dive later. Note that the first dive affects even this
group designation. A dive of 71 minutes to 50 feet would go into
group J if no prior dive had been made.

These calculations may seem difficult for the first few problems
you attempt, but learning the system is worthwhile. In the above
example, the repetitive dive system permitted 71 minutes at 50
feet, while adding bottom time allowed only 10 minutes.

A whole series of dives can be made repeating the steps above.
After another 2 hours on the surface, our diver would be in group
G. This would add 56 minutes to another 50 foot dive and permit
only 44 minutes actual bottom time.

Another use of the repetitive dive system is determining required surface intervals to avoid decompression stops, when dives
of predetermined length and depth are planned.

A photographer wants to work at 90 feet for 20 minutes. Then
he wants to be able to dive to 60 feet for 40 minutes. How long
must he stay on the surface between these dives? The problem is

TABLE 2

RESIDUAL NITROGEN TIMETABLE FOR REPETITIVE AIR DIVES

Dives following surface intervals of more than 12 hours are not repetitive dives. Use actual bottom times in the Standard Air Decompression Tables to compute decompression for such dives.

Repetitive group at the beginning of the surface interval (rows) → surface interval range (h:min) → *New Group Designation* (columns).

Beginning group	A	B	C	D	E	F	G	H	I	J	K	L	M	N	O	Z
A	0:10–12:00															
B	2:11–12:00	0:10–2:10														
C	2:50–12:00	1:40–2:49	0:10–1:39													
D	5:49–12:00	2:39–5:48	1:10–2:38	0:10–1:09												
E	6:33–12:00	3:23–6:32	1:58–3:22	0:55–1:57	0:10–0:54											
F	7:06–12:00	3:58–7:05	2:29–3:57	1:30–2:28	0:46–1:29	0:10–0:45										
G	7:36–12:00	4:26–7:35	2:59–4:25	2:00–2:58	1:16–1:59	0:41–1:15	0:10–0:40									
H	8:00–12:00	4:50–7:59	3:21–4:49	2:24–3:20	1:42–2:23	1:07–1:41	0:37–1:06	0:10–0:36								
I	8:22–12:00	5:13–8:21	3:44–5:12	2:45–3:43	2:03–2:44	1:30–2:02	1:00–1:29	0:34–0:59	0:10–0:33							
J	8:41–12:00	5:41–8:40	4:03–5:40	3:05–4:02	2:21–3:04	1:48–2:20	1:20–1:47	0:55–1:19	0:32–0:54	0:10–0:31						
K	8:59–12:00	5:49–8:58	4:20–5:48	3:22–4:19	2:39–3:21	2:04–2:38	1:36–2:03	1:12–1:35	0:50–1:11	0:29–0:49	0:10–0:28					
L	9:13–12:00	6:03–9:12	4:36–6:02	3:37–4:35	2:54–3:36	2:20–2:53	1:50–2:19	1:26–1:49	1:05–1:25	0:46–1:04	0:27–0:45	0:10–0:26				
M	9:29–12:00	6:19–9:28	4:50–6:18	3:53–4:49	3:09–3:52	2:35–3:08	2:06–2:34	1:40–2:05	1:19–1:39	1:00–1:18	0:43–0:59	0:26–0:42	0:10–0:25			
N	9:44–12:00	6:33–9:43	5:04–6:32	4:05–5:03	3:23–4:04	2:48–3:22	2:19–2:47	1:54–2:18	1:31–1:53	1:12–1:30	0:55–1:11	0:40–0:54	0:25–0:39	0:10–0:24		
O	9:55–12:00	6:45–9:54	5:17–6:44	4:18–5:16	3:34–4:17	3:00–3:33	2:30–2:59	2:05–2:29	1:44–2:04	1:25–1:43	1:08–1:24	0:52–1:07	0:37–0:51	0:24–0:36	0:10–0:23	
Z	10:06–12:00	6:57–10:05	5:28–6:56	4:30–5:27	3:46–4:29	3:11–3:45	2:43–3:10	2:18–2:42	1:56–2:17	1:37–1:55	1:19–1:36	1:03–1:18	0:49–1:02	0:35–0:48	0:23–0:34	0:10–0:22

New Group Designation

TABLE 3

RESIDUAL NITROGEN TIME (MINUTES)

REPETITIVE DIVE DEPTH	257	241	213	187	161	138	116	101	87	73	61	49	37	25	17	7
40	257	241	213	187	161	138	116	101	87	73	61	49	37	25	17	7
50	169	160	142	124	111	99	87	76	66	56	47	38	29	21	13	6
60	122	117	107	97	88	79	70	61	52	44	36	30	24	17	11	5
70	100	96	87	80	72	64	57	50	43	37	31	26	20	15	9	4
80	84	80	73	68	61	54	48	43	38	32	28	23	18	13	8	4
90	73	70	64	58	53	47	43	38	33	29	24	20	16	11	7	3
100	64	62	57	52	48	43	38	34	30	26	22	18	14	10	7	3
110	57	55	51	47	42	38	34	31	27	24	20	16	13	10	6	3
120	52	50	46	43	39	35	32	28	25	21	18	15	12	9	6	3
130	46	44	40	38	35	31	28	25	22	19	16	13	11	8	6	3
140	42	40	38	35	32	29	26	23	20	18	15	12	10	7	5	2
150	40	38	35	32	30	27	24	22	19	17	14	12	9	7	5	2
160	37	36	33	31	28	26	23	20	18	16	13	11	9	6	4	2
170	35	34	31	29	26	24	22	19	17	15	13	10	8	6	4	2
180	32	31	29	27	25	22	20	18	16	14	12	10	8	6	4	2
190	31	30	28	26	24	21	19	17	15	13	11	10	8	6	4	2

illustrated on the accompanying worksheet. The depth and actual bottom time of the second dive is known. At 60 feet, permissable total bottom time is 60 minutes. Thus, the diver could have a penalty time of up to 20 minutes and make this a 40 minute dive.

REPETITIVE DIVE WORKSHEET

First dive

depth __*90 ft.*__   **repetitive group** __*F*__

bottom
time __*20 min.*__   from "no decompression"
                                       table

Surface interval

2 hours 29 minutes   (from residual nitrogen
                                       timetable)
beginning group __*F*__

new group __*C*__

Second dive   (from residual nitrogen
                                       timetable)
depth __*60 ft.*__

residual nitro-
gen time __*17 min.*__   **new repetitive group** __*J*__

bottom time __*40 min.*__
                                       from "no decompression"
total time __*57 min.*__   table

Group C is the repetitive group that comes closest to adding 20 minutes penalty time to a 60 foot dive. After the 90 minute dive, the photographer was in group F. By finding the intersection of group F and C columns on table 2, we find that the minimum surface interval would be 2 hours 29 minutes for the photographer.

This example also illustrates how quickly the decompression requirements increase. A dive of 10 minutes to 90 feet would go into group C. It could be followed by a dive to 60 feet for 40 minutes after only a 10 minute surface interval. Adding 10 minutes to the first dive added 2 hours and 19 minutes to the surface interval.

Generally, it saves time to take the deeper of two dives first. If we reversed the situation above and first went to 60 feet for 40 minutes, the repetitive group would be G. A surface interval of 2 hours and 29 minutes would shift the group to D, which adds 16 minutes to our desired 90 foot dive. The planned bottom time of 20 minutes plus this 16 minute penalty time would give an actual bottom time of 36 minutes, which violates "no decompression" standards. To make this a conforming dive would require a drop in repetitive groups from G to B that would add 7 minutes to actual bottom time. This shift takes a minimum of 4 hours and 26 minutes. As just illustrated, *a little planning can save a lot of time.* The time differences relate to the tissues affected and the degree of saturation which occurs in short, deep dives versus longer, shallower ones.

The tables become impractical only for dives of a similar depth separated by very short intervals. A dive to 60 feet for 30 minutes enters group F. A surface interval of 40 minutes does not shift the group, so you start the repetitive dive to 60 feet with a penalty of 36 minutes. This is longer than the actual bottom time for the first dive: a physiological impossibility. Here a savings would be afforded by adding the bottom time of the first 60 foot dive to that of the second. You may always add bottom time, if the decompression is then calculated as though the whole dive was made at the deeper depth.

SCUBA DIVING AND DECOMPRESSION TABLES

Standard decompression tables generally work well. Interest exists in improving them for several reasons. They are hard to understand, and using the tables, especially the repetitive ones, requires dive planning. More importantly, the tables are more suited to hard hat than scuba diving.

Bubbles sometimes form after an apparently safe dive. Tables could be redesigned and then tested using bubble detection rather than symptoms as the criterion of correctness. In one program, this would increase the decompression requirement in long, shallow dives and decrease it for short, deep dives. It is relatively easy to compute tables which look appealing. The problem is in validation. Because of the wide individual variability in bubble formation and decompression sickness, large numbers of exposures must be made to establish a table's safety. The Navy's tables have a good safety record over many years. Most decompression sickness cases result from diver errors rather than table failures.

Divers should not try to modify the Navy tables. Slowing ascents and adding shallow stops have no verified value. In fact, current research suggests that deep stops may be more valuable than shallow ones.

The tables do take a little getting used to. This is a currently unavoidable requirement for safe scuba diving. Planning is necessary. With practice, the tables are not hard to use.

The biggest drawback of the tables is their poor applicability to typical scuba diving. Hard hat divers generally work at one depth during a dive. Scuba divers typically go to several depths on one dive. Decompression principles require that the whole dive be considered as occurring at the deepest point. A diver who spends 10 minutes at 60 feet, 5 minutes at 80 feet, and 25 minutes at 40 feet must treat the dive as 40 minutes at 80 feet. This is clearly very conservative. There is, unfortunately, no acceptable way to avoid the restriction. It is dangerous to try to average depths or times in an effort to reduce decompression requirements.

Some attempts have been made to assign depth time equivalents so that a planned multilevel dive could be made while accounting for the varying nitrogen uptakes at different depths. This new system attempts to establish equivalents so that more time in shallow depths could be counted the same as less time in deeper ranges. The equivalents for the total dive are summed to determine decompression requirements. This new system has three serious drawbacks:

a. It still requires careful planning and monitoring of depths and durations.

b. It will not work well for a dive going to many levels randomly.

c. It is not based on correct assumptions.

The first two objections are real, but manageable. The third makes the system useless and dangerous. The multilevel system assumes that equivalent gas uptakes and elimination can be determined. This is not true. All decompression systems are based on models of the body. When actual measurements are made, it is often found that these models are imperfect. In theory, gas uptake rate should be equal to gas elimination at a given depth. Actually, the rates are not equal and the degree of inequality is unpredictable. This is true for individual organs as well as for the total body. The multilevel system depends on calculations based on false assumptions.

Diving in the Mountains

Divers visiting mountain lakes have special decompression problems. The decreased air pressure means that after a dive in the mountains, the air/water nitrogen pressure gradient is larger than after an ocean dive to the same depth. This increases the risk of bubble formation. Fresh water density is less than salt and this partially offsets the effect of the reduced atmospheric pressure.

Three basic approaches have been used in high altitude diving:

a. to compute new tables

b. to use standard tables correcting the depth to correspond to the altitude.

c. to dive with a capillary depth gauge and use standard tables

The computation of new tables has the problem common to any new table: *validation of safety*. The Swiss have devised new tables but they are not in widespread use in the United States.

In the second approach, the differences in water density and atmospheric pressure are used to calculate a "theoretical ocean depth" which should compare with the actual altitude dive in decompression requirements. As an example, a dive to 100 feet at an elevation of 6,000 feet is the same as an ocean dive to 122 feet. Then this theoretical dive is used in the standard Navy decompression tables. Ascent rates can also be corrected for altitude. It is not possible to calculate decompression stops accurately using this simple system.

No actual details of altitude correction are given here, since they are not truly validated. They have theoretical support but still must be considered "untested."

Using a capillary gauge eliminates the need to correct for depth. These gauges read "deep" at high altitudes and thus automatically correct for the reduced atmospheric pressure. Readings from a capillary gauge can be used directly with standard tables.

Upon arriving at a mountain lake, the diver has excess nitrogen remaining from his life at sea level. The Swiss tables correct for this. When using any other system at least twelve hours should pass before diving so that the first dive is not a repetitive one.

Altitude diving requires special knowledge and no one should attempt it without study and preparation.

Flying After Diving

Going up in a plane after a scuba dive increases the pressure gradient of nitrogen and may cause bubbling and decompression sickness. Even commercial planes are not pressurized to sea level. Depending on the airline and route, cabin pressure may vary from 6,000 to 8,000 feet.

Because of this reduced pressure, scuba divers should not fly immediately after surfacing. Again, there are several unproven ways of determining the safe time interval before flying. These depend on the depth and duration of the dive. Because of the uncertainty in decompression, it is better not to push the limits. For safety, an interval of twelve hours is advisable with twenty-four hours if the dive required decompression stops.

Decompression Meters

In the dream world of scuba diving, there are no decompression tables. A handy device tells the diver when he should surface and when he can dive again. There would be no more artificial limitations in multilevel diving and no repetitive dive calculations.

This dream piece of equipment would be a computer that calculates and balances nitrogen uptake and elimination in coordination with safe decompression principles.

Actually, a primitive decompression meter has been available for several years, but it is far from ideal. Its design premise is not based on any widely accepted decompression model. It most certainly does not follow the Navy program. The meter is more conservative than the Navy in shallow depths to 60 feet and then much more permissive in deep water. This is unfortunate because it is the deep ranges of decompression limits which are most dangerous. The meter is most widely used for deep diving and this is where the meter works poorly. The repetitive dive capacity of the meter is extremely poor. Recent changes in operating instructions have not made the meter any better. Used by itself, the meter is not a safe way to avoid decompression sickness.

13

First Aid for Decompression Sickness

Decompression sickness may occur despite adherence to accepted diving standards. The planning of a scuba dive must then include a consideration of what to do in the event of a decompression accident.

Before the dive begins a series of questions must be answered.

a. Are the divers familiar with common symptoms of decompression sickness?

b. If, despite the proper use of decompression schedules, symptoms do develop, where is the nearest treatment chamber? (The location may be obtained from the Coast Guard or by calling the Navy's Experimental Diving Unit in Panama City, Florida.)

c. Is the nearest chamber functional?

d. Does the chamber have a staff on duty or on call?

e. How can a physician, familiar with diving medicine, be contacted?

f. What is the safest and most efficient way to transport a sick diver to the recompression chamber?

This checklist can be used to supplement the ones that apply to general first aid and to the care of the severely injured diver.

MAKING A DIAGNOSIS

Failure to realize that a diver has decompression sickness is the biggest hindrance to treatment. The almost universal response is to blame the symptoms on fatigue, muscle stress, or trauma.

Decompression sickness typically has a rather gradual onset and

115

initially may not seem serious. The occurrences of any of the following symptoms in a scuba diver are strongly suggestive of decompression sickness. Symptoms include tingling or sensations of "pins and needles," numbness, weakness, pain in arms or legs, and particularly in the joints, skin rash or itching, and respiratory difficulty or unconsciousness. The latter is unlikely to be part of decompression sickness unless there has been an uncontrolled ascent. Most frequently decompression sickness symptoms occur within one hour of surfacing, but they can be delayed. Rarely, the disease appears twenty-four hours after the dive. The slower onset and generally milder signs help differentiate decompression sickness from air embolism.

Limb pain is a common complaint. In distinguishing between bends and trauma, it may be useful to note whether the diver remembers injuring himself. Unfortunately, in the excitement of a dive, it is easy to ignore a bump on the knee or a twisted hand. Simple injuries may have local signs such as bleeding, swelling, discoloration, or tenderness. These are usually absent in decompression sickness.

Divers often make the mistake of ignoring mild symptoms or try to treat symptoms with aspirin or alcohol. A minor symptom should be a warning that decompression sickness has taken place. Not infrequently, serious involvement, such as nerve damage, develops more slowly than simple pain. *When in doubt, treat.*

Initial Therapy

When the diagnosis has been made or seriously considered, the recompression chamber should be contacted. This gives the facility time to prepare for treatment and provides an opportunity for consultation.

Be prepared to give information about the dive the victim made, his symptoms, and general condition. Occasionally, chambers are run without a diving physician in attendance. It would be wise to contact a physician trained in diving medicine so that he may assist in planning the proper treatment.

Transportation should be made efficiently, since delays in the treatment increase the likelihood of permanent damage. If far from shore, divers may contact the Coast Guard for air evacuation. When the chamber is not too far away, land transportation will be easiest to arrange. Obviously, less speed is required for a diver with wrist pain than for a paralyzed diver, but that does not excuse avoidable delays in mild cases.

If the chamber is distant, a helicopter or airplane should be employed. Altitude worsens decompression sickness by increasing bubble size, so pressurized cabins and low flying are important.

When available, let the patient breathe oxygen through a mask. This increases the elimination of body nitrogen and provides added oxygen for damaged tissues. On expedition-type dives, oxygen bottles are a valuable part of the first aid kit.

During transportation the diver should be kept warm and rested. In decompression sickness position is probably not extremely important, but the supine position with the legs above the head may cause any migrating bubbles to go toward the feet rather than toward the head.

Do not give any medicines without medical advice as these may complicate the subsequent evaluation of the diver's condition. Alcohol should not be given. If a physician or paramedic is available to start an intravenous infusion, this is valuable in improving blood flow through the small vessels.

Definitive Treatment

Recompression is the basis of therapy for decompression sickness as previously discussed. When started promptly, therapy has a high success rate. When treatment is delayed, the failure rate rises sharply.

Direct contact with the recompression facility is stressed, since this lessens the time from surfacing to treatment. Unfortunately, many hospital emergency rooms are not oriented toward the recognition and treatment of diving accidents. When divers are taken to these rooms, improper treatment may be given in addition to postponing definitve treatment. Diving accident reports often contain statements such as "patient was in emergency room for twelve hours before contact was made with the recompression chamber." Until diving emergency procedures are more widely understood among the general hospital populace, it is best for divers to contact treatment centers themselves. (When other injuries are present, however, it may be advisable to stop first at a hospital emergency room.)

When the divers have transported the stricken diver to a proper chamber and treatment has begun, their contribution to therapy ends. Now is the time to analyze the accident with the intention of preventing recurrences on future dives. The process of first aid, as well as the transportation, should be critiqued.

Portable Chambers

Small, one-person recompression chambers are available which can be transported on diving trips. These can be valuable by providing almost immediate recompression. However, they are not without certain, serious drawbacks. Ideally, these should be used to provide recompression support during transportation to a large chamber. A portable chamber should be chosen which will either fit inside a big chamber or which can be mated with the big chamber.

Actual treatment in a portable, one-person chamber is desirable only if no other chamber can be reached because the diving is done in such a remote area. Small chambers do not provide access to the patient. This prevents supportive care such as resuscitation, long term intravenous fluid administration, or drug administration. Treatment with air is not as effective as with oxygen and may require more pressure than the chamber can tolerate. On the other hand, using oxygen introduces the hazards of fire and oxygen poisoning both of which are dangerous to an isolated patient. A long treatment will use up a lot of compressed air.

The most serious issue in treatment in portable chambers is that treatment is limited to recompression. More and more therapists are using other modalities such as Dextran, steroids, plasma, and heparin. Treatment involves much more than turning on the air.

In the field it is easy to fail to note any early neurological sign which is masked by severe elbow pain, for example. This leads to the choice of the wrong treatment table which increases the possibility of permanent damage.

A particularly unhappy instance of portable chamber therapy supervised by non-medical personnel involved a young Naval officer in Hawaii. After a routine dive he developed leg weakness and was promptly pressurized. He recovered quickly and the diving supervisor decompressed the chamber. The diver was all right for a few minutes but then the symptoms returned. He was again compressed but on a table designed for minor symptoms. Finally he was transported to a proper chamber and treated correctly. Even after two sessions on the major table, he had leg paralysis and no bladder function. Fortunately, he made a gradual recovery over the next month.

The planning and execution of therapy is not always as simple as described in books.

Recompression Chamber

Water Recompression

Water recompression is a very popular maneuver by poorly informed divers. Sometimes this is used as a "trial of pressure." For example, a diver with shoulder pain is resubmerged to see if the pressure makes his pain go away. This sounds good, but usually only confuses things since it is not easy to evaluate pain relief in the water. It is uncertain how deep to go or how long to stay. This trial, of course, is actually a repetitive dive which makes decompression sickness more likely later. A pressure trial in a chamber sometimes is useful when a diving physician is unsure of the diagnosis. Properly done, it involves twenty minutes of oxygen breathing at sixty feet. If there is absolutely no change in the symptoms, they are probably not due to decompression sickness.

Attempts to actually treat decompression sickness by water recompression are much worse than water trials. Some of the problems associated with this technique include:

a. Treatment with air has limited effectiveness at best.

b. Even the shortest air treatment table takes six hours and requires a starting depth of 100 feet.

c. Supplying sufficient air for six hours would be difficult.

d. Depth control is difficult.

e. Water gets cold before six hours are up.

f. Rough seas frequently develop.

g. The victim is likely to be seriously fatigued.

h. Communication with the victim is difficult.

i. There is no good way to take care of a sick diver underwater.

j. A pressure exposure is actually another dive and may cause decompression sickness itself.

k. Attempts at water therapy delay transportation and proper therapy.

Water treatment is not good. The time would be much better spent transporting the victim to a recompression facility. Once recompression begins, it should not be interrupted until treatment is complete.

A careful plan in case of decompression sickness will greatly aid in the efficient treatment of a diver, should the need arise.

14

Nitrogen Narcosis

The fol'owing letter comes form the mailbag of "Super Instructor" who writes a popular advice column for divers.

"I have what seems to me is a strange problem. When I go diving the first few minutes seem hard, with getting my equipment and getting into the water. We mostly dive in murky water and it is sort of scary going down. My ears usually hurt, too. But at about 70 feet things get better. We usually dive between 70 and 100 feet for lobsters. I really enjoy it, but then when we start back up, I get apprehensive again. I can't understand why I like it better deep than shallow. Is there something wrong with me?"

A significant part of this diver's fondness for the deep results from the narcotic effects of breathing compressed air. The nitrogen in air causes changes in the brain. Nitrogen is an inert gas which means that it is not metabolized in the body. "Inert" definitely does not mean inactive. Other inert gases such as argon, krypton, and xenon have similar actions.

Effects of Narcosis

Narcosis from nitrogen can best be compared to the effects of breathing general anesthetics. These cause amnesia, analgesia, excitement, and finally unconsciousness. Anesthetics probably act by somehow modifying membrane properties in the central nervous system. Potency is most reliably related to solubility of the gas in fat. Nitrogen is insoluble in comparison to anesthetics. For example, its lipid solubility is 28 times less than nitrous oxide, the weakest anesthetic in common use. As the dose of inert gas increases, the body absorbs more and the effects of the gas intensify. During diving, high pressure raises the effective dose of nitrogen, although its concentration remains 79 percent by increasing the nitrogen partial pressure. Just as in decompression sickness, the direct effect of pressure causes indirect effects by increasing nitrogen absorption.

There is no reason to think that nitrogen narcosis acts differently from anesthetics. Small concentrations of nitrous oxide cause decreased pain sensation, then excitement and delirium. The name "laughing gas" comes from nitrous oxide's suppression of inhibitory brain centers which can lead to euphoria and laughing. Higher concentrations of anesthetics cause unconsciousness and non-responsiveness to pain. Death results at toxic doses from cardiovascular or respiratory depression.

Nitrogen breathing in diving follows characteristic patterns. Initially the diver notices mood changes—usually things appear more pleasant. Apprehension and attentiveness fade. A group of Navy physicians made a narcosis familiarization run in a large pressure chamber to 250 feet. Despite the usual earaches, the descent was rapid. Outside control reported "on the bottom" and the inside supervisor acknowledged "on the bottom." His speech was distorted by the high pressure air so his gruff boatswain's mate voice sounded like Donald Duck. This started 12 physicians giggling and the laughing did not stop during the 10 minutes at 250 feet.

Following mood changes, conceptual reasoning becomes impaired. Next reaction time increases. Manual dexterity is affected last. By the time clumsiness is apparent, divers may have gone too deep. The insidious nature of narcosis makes it deadly. If clumsiness appeared early, the diver would recognize he had gone too far and turn back. But narcosis feels good. It begins before a person can detect it, even if he is trying to observe its effects. Sophisticated tests reveal changes as shallow as 60 feet, while most people appear normal to 100 feet.

At about 100 feet, impairment becomes significant. It progresses steadily and will end in unconsciousness below 300 feet. At these extreme depths, oxygen poisoning becomes likely. Scuba diving is dangerous below 110 to 125 feet, since there is little control over a free swimming diver. Hard hat work can be done somewhat deeper because an injured diver can be hauled up.

At 200 feet a hard hat student could stop singing, "I'm forever blowing bubbles" long enough to recite his serial number and do a few simple calculations. When the questions stopped, he resumed singing and dancing. This typifies diver behavior during narcosis. Only by hard concentration can simple tasks be completed. When work must be done underwater, the tasks must be planned before the dive, so that the diver has a pattern of behavior. Otherwise, he may concentrate on screwing down a plate, but forget to breathe while doing so!

People vary widely in their susceptibility to nitrogen narcosis. There is some suggestion that those who are tolerant to alcohol are also tolerant to nitrogen. This is not well established and does not excuse deep diving. It may be that variation is due more to familiarity with diving. Comparisons of equivalent pressure exposures in open water and in dry pressure chambers have demonstrated more impairment of manual dexterity in the water. This suggests a contribution of anxiety. Experienced divers usually can work better in narcotizing depths than novices. The existence of true adaptation to narcosis has not been proven. Quite possibly, the improved function is due to lower anxiety and an ability to concentrate better on assigned tasks.

Carbon dioxide retention also adds to narcosis. In open circuit scuba, this should not be a problem, except for divers who excessively skip breathe.

Preventing Narcosis

Narcosis is a problem for recreational and commerical divers because it severely limits the depth of diving. Commercial diving substitutes less narcotic mixes for air. The most common substitute is helium with oxygen. Helium is not narcotic even at the deepest depths tested. However, at high pressures helium causes a muscle tremor state known as the high pressure neurological syndrome. Interestingly, this can be minimized by the use of very small quantities of nitrogen in the helium/oxygen mixture.

For recreational diving the only prevention for nitrogen narcosis is the avoidance of deep diving. There simply is not any way to make a safe, deep scuba dive. Even experts have perished because of narcosis. No one should count on being tolerant of narcosis, or capable of functioning in spite of it. No one can be sure how he will react at a given depth.

Many factors interact in narcosis. Any condition that hurts mental function will intensify nitrogen narcosis. Drugs, including such apparently harmless ones as decongestants and seasickness pills, may be a problem. Cold water distracts attention and may intensify the loss of alertness. Fatigue also affects underwater performance and will supplement the impairment by narcosis. Alcohol increases the likeihood of narcosis. Alcohol and nitrogen effects act together on the brain. Thus, an amount of alcohol which appears to have no effect while on the surface may cause narcosis in relatively shallow depths.

Prevention of nitrogen narcosis requires adherence to these principles:

a. Dive only when physically and mentally fit.

b. Avoid drinking even small amounts of alcohol before diving.

c. Medicines should not be used in diving except after careful testing.

d. Wear and use an accurate depth gauge.

e. If diving in deep water, as in sea cliffs, plan how deep you will go and do not change your plans once in the water.

f. Do not count on your buddy to keep you out of trouble. He may be equally narcotized.

Treatment of narcosis involves coming back to shallow water. The narcosis fades as quickly as it begins. By itself, narcosis will not cause deaths in scuba diving, but it kills by leading to drowning. If a deep diver requires rescue, be prepared to provide prompt resuscitation. Be very careful in trying to retrieve divers who have gone too far. In several cases, the rescuer has been incapacitated and killed while making a deep rescue dive.

15

Oxygen Poisoning

The body uses only a small part of the oxygen inhaled in every breath. This makes mouth-to-mouth resuscitation possible because exhaled air contains 16 percent oxygen; inhaled air contains 21 percent oxygen. On land this wasting of oxygen is unimportant because there is plenty of air. But in diving, the exhausting of over 75 percent of every breath becomes significant as it drastically reduces duration of air supply.

The air could be rebreathed except that exhaled air contains high concentrations of carbon dioxide which would quickly become toxic. Cycling exhalation through carbon dioxide absorbant chemicals makes rebreathing safe. If pure oxygen is used in the tank, duration is increased even more. This discovery led many early divers to make their own oxygen rebreathers. Many accidents followed because improper use can cause poisoning from carbon dioxide, low oxygen, or high oxygen.

With proper technique the problems of carbon dioxide and low oxygen can be solved. But, poisoning from excessive amounts of oxygen limits diving depth and duration. Although we must have oxygen to live, too much oxygen can be harmful. Oxygen can poison all the organs of the body. Despite intensive investigation, the mechanism of oxygen poisoning has not been determined. It is a very basic process because all plants and animals are susceptible to it. Severe enzyme systems have been implicated. Perhaps the syndrome results from interacting mechanisms rather than from a single one.

Sensitivity to oxygen varies among the different organ systems. The lungs and central nervous system are the two most frequently affected organs. Oxygen effects depend on the concentration inhaled, atmospheric pressure, and the length of exposure. At elevated pressures, as in diving, a smaller concentration becomes toxic. (The physiologic effects depend on oxygen partial pressure which is the product of total pressure and percent concentration oxygen.) It takes time for oxygen poisoning to become evident and this period is shortened at high pressures.

Lung poisoning requires several hours of exposure and is not an issue for scuba divers. The danger of lung poisoning limits the applicability of hyperbaric oxygen therapy and is an important factor in saturation diving.

Short exposures to pure oxygen at slightly elevated pressures quickly poison the central nervous system. Even on dives shallower than 33 feet, pure oxygen breathing can cause convulsions. Other symptoms frequently precede oxygen convulsions. Excessive oxygen may cause nausea, vertigo, visual disturbances, restlessness, and irritability. Muscle twitching, especially of the facial muscles often occurs. Convulsions may start without warning.

Oxygen convulsions have the characteristics of grand mal epilepsy. The victim first enters a rigid "tonic" phase and loses consciousness. His breathing stops, but this will not cause hypoxia since his tissue oxygen levels are high. After about 30 seconds, the "clonic" phase begins with contraction of the head and neck, trunk, and limbs. Typically this ends within a minute and then breathing begins as the victim regains consciousness. He may have no memory for the time immediately before the convulsion.

A single convulsion causes no permanent damage by itself. If a diver can be promptly retrieved he will recover. Obviously, a convulsing diver may drown before he can be helped.

Several factors affect the likelihood of central nervous oxygen toxicity. These include exercise, carbon dioxide retention, wet versus dry, and individual susceptibility.

Exercise drastically reduces oxygen tolerance. Swimming divers have had convulsions after shorter and shallower exposures than are tolerated at rest. Operationally, divers are usually limited to 75 minutes at 25 feet with a maximum of 40 feet for 10 minutes. Standard hyperbaric therapy utilizes exposures equal to 66 feet for periods of up to two hours. Exercise even without carbon dioxide retention intensifies oxygen toxicity. Carbon dioxide accumulation lowers the threshold for oxygen poisoning. This may occur in poorly ventilated hard hats or in scuba divers who breathe improperly.

Actual water exposures cause more poisoning than equivalent chamber pressurizations. This is true even when exercise and ventilation are the same in both groups.

People vary widely in their tolerances to oxygen. The Navy attempts to detect sensitive individuals by giving all diving candidates an oxygen tolerance test which requires pure oxygen breathing at 60 feet for 30 minutes. Those who have symptoms of toxicity are eliminated from all diving training. Unfortunately passing this test does not guarantee that a person will not have problems with high pressure oxygen later on. Oxygen tolerance varies from day to day.

Oxygen poisoning should never be a problem in recreational diving. The occasional bends victim will receive oxygen therapy, but this is generally well tolerated. Interruptions of the oxygen exposure by short periods of air breathing increase tolerance.

Oxygen scuba is not useful except for very specialized use. The depth restrictions and need for elaborate equipment make it very impractical.

Air can be breathed to depths of almost 300 feet before its oxygen concentration reaches the two atmospheres absolute which can cause acute oxygen poisoning. Long before this, the scuba diver will be incapacitated by nitrogen narcosis.

Oxygen breathing divers must be shifted to air if symptoms of oxygen toxicity appear. This is difficult if the scuba diver is only using a pure oxygen system. Ascent during a convulsion is dangerous because the victim does not breathe and may suffer lung rupture and air embolism. The main goals are to protect the diver during a seizure and to bring him to the surface when the seizure stops.

16

The Lure of the Deep

How deep have you gone? Every diver hears that question from his impressionable friends. After reading about willowy models effortlessly exploring wrecks at 200 feet, it is no surprise that many novices want to go deep. For the diver, the number of feet dived seems to have a mystical value.

The popularity of deep scuba diving waxes and wanes. In its infancy deep diving records were widely publicized, but after the dangers became recognized through the deaths of prominent divers, interest faded. Skin diving magazines and organizations stopped promoting these escapades and began to discuss the risks. Recently, deep diving has regained much of its stature. Dive clubs promote deep diving instruction, and a deep diving program is presented at a national training conference.

There are obvious good reasons for deep diving. These include geologic and biologic exploration, salvage, construction and military work. Trying to set records is foolish. The highest mountains can be climbed, but the deepest reaches of the ocean will never be touched by any free diver. How impressive is it to go to 250 feet when most of the ocean is many times deeper?

Under the best of circumstances, the problems of diving increase with depth. Many of the limitations in professional diving develop from attempts to extend the working range. Even with exotic mixed gases, intensive training, and superb support facilities, the ocean's barriers often cannot be breached. For the air breathing scuba diver the problems quickly become insurmountable.

How deep is deep for a scuba diver? A novice is deep when he exceeds the depth he could reach on a breathhold dive. The more experienced diver has no definite depth level. For purposes of discussion, the U.S. Navy's standard scuba limit of 125 feet is reasonable. However, 100 feet may be too deep for many people.

Getting down is not a problem if the diver can clear his ears and sinuses. As water pressure compresses his suit, he loses buoyancy and heads down. The challenges await at depth and on ascent. Very quickly the scuba diver finds his air supply is low.

The standard 70 cubic foot tank (fully charged) supplies 70 cubic feet of air on the surface. Its output decreases to 35 cubic feet at 33 feet (2 atmospheres absolute) and to 17½ at 99 feet (4 atmospheres). Assuming an average air consumption of one cubic foot each minute, a diver can calculate how long a tank will last at any depth. The dedicated deep diver uses larger twin tanks, but even the old twin 90s supply last less than 30 minutes if most of it is spent at 230 feet. This provides little reserve for a complicated ascent.

Most people will not want to stay very long in the deep, since conditions are not usually too pleasant. Visibility decreases as do the natural communications between divers. Below about 70 feet the warming effect of the sun is lost; this combines with wet suit compression to make cold a serious problem. Cold increases metabolic rate thus increasing air consumption. The impaired muscle coordination resulting from chilling makes work difficult and may restrict the ability to use equipment.

The modern scuba regulator works well to depths greater than those usually attained. Breathing is restricted somewhat as water pressure increases. This could be a problem with an old or poorly maintained regulator. An unfit diver may have severe breathing problems while exerting in deep water. If the regulator does malfunction or the tank runs dry, ascent risks increase. Quite possibly the buddy diver will be low on air and both divers may be too confused for calm action. An octopus rig saves sharing a regulator, but it does not prolong air supply. A pony bottle can supply extra air, if the diver is coherent and coordinated enough to turn it on.

Emergency ascents can be made from any scuba depth but they become more challenging with depth. A swimming ascent, with regulator held in the mouth to provide any breaths from remaining tank air, is the safest technique, if buddy or octopus breathing are impossible. It will work, if the diver remains calm and has normal lungs. The buoyancy vest will not provide much lift as the ascent begins and then it may provide uncontrollable amounts of lift.

The leading cause of death in deep diving is nitrogen narcosis.

Its insidious nature renders divers nonfunctional before they realize they are in trouble. Nitrogen narcosis leads to irrational behavior and makes it impossible to deal with emergencies. Typically a lost diver is last seen headed peacefully past 250 feet on his way to the bottom. People vary widely in their susceptibility to nitrogen narcosis but no one is immune.

The effects begin before the diver notes any changes in his mental state or coordination—at about 100 feet. Because of its subtle onset the diver may never recognize that he is affected, or he may recognize it too late for recovery. The buddy system provides no protection since both divers may be equally afflicted. Since susceptibility to narcosis varies for each individual, there is no way to predict what depth is dangerous for a given person. A well-trained, experienced diver can work at depths that would incapacitate a jittery novice. But even experienced divers underestimate the potency of nitrogen. It is best to avoid determining the nature of narcosis.

The other major component of air—oxygen—also poisons the body at high pressures. Central nervous system symptoms, including convulsions, follow when oxygen pressures are two atmospheres or greater. This pressure of oxygen is achieved when air is breathed at a depth of 300 feet in the ocean. Most divers would be so narcotized at this depth that they would never notice oxygen poisoning. But a diver could easily be lost if he had an oxygen convulsion deep in the sea.

Decompression sickness severely restricts professional deep diving. It makes deep scuba diving especially hazardous. As discussed in the chapters on decompression sickness, the safest dives avoid the need for decompression stops. For deep diving this is virtually impossible as the permitted bottom time for "no decompression" dives between 150 and 190 feet are five minutes and the tables do not permit dives below 190 feet.

With a normal descent this allows, in reality, no time to enjoy the maximum depth. Air supply of a single tank severly limits dive time, but supply time exceeds "no decompression" limits below about 110 feet. Exceeding "no decompression" standards presents two serious problems: the risk of decompression sickness and providing air for decompression stops. The "no decompression" tables have the lowest incidence of decompression sickness and the table safety decreases as dives become more extreme.

Decompression stops are not easy to arrange in sport scuba

diving. A look at the Navy Standard Tables shows how quickly ascent time becomes prolonged.

The major difficulites in arranging decompressions stops are:

a. Providing adequate air for the ascent.

b. Accurate timing of stops and ascent times.

c. Reliable depth markers: stops on a rope may swing widely with wave actions.

d. Arranging safety divers to manage air supplies and supervise the ascents.

e. Communication with dive boat and fellow divers.

f. Temperature maintenance, especially a problem since decompression stops are to be taken at rest.

g. Weather or sea state changes that make it necessary to shorten the dive.

It seems simple to keep track of dive time and depth. Unfortunately mistakes, be they human or from equipment, are often made in these measurements. In deep diving even a slight miscalculation may cause decompression sickness. Decompression meters are often used in deep diving as a safety backup. Unfortunately, the available meters are particularly dangerous in the deep ranges. They permit longer stays than the standard tables.

With all these problems attendant to deep diving, how can safe expeditions be made? Commercial and Navy divers don't even try. They use mixed gases to prevent narcosis and may use surface decompression chambers. Elaborate club or class efforts can reduce the risk and may even make moderately deep diving (to 125 feet) fairly safe. People who love to dive for deeper wrecks definitely take a risk. The penalty for a mistake or misfortune is serious. Deep diving requires the ultimate in skill at a time when skill is not ultimate.

About the Author

Christopher Dueker began diving in the United States Navy where he trained at the Navy's School of Submarine Medicine and the School for Deep Sea Divers in Washington, D.C. He currently dives for recreation, and is a frequent speaker at diving club meetings throughout California. Dueker also lectures for the Diving Safety Digest, a series of cassette tapes aimed at educating divers, and participates regularly in the Sonoma County Diving Rescue Workshops. He is also a member of the Undersea Medical Society, versed in all aspects of professional and recreational diving.

Dueker is a graduate of Pomona College and the U.S.C. Medical School, presently in private practice as an anesthesiologist at the Palo Alto Medical Center. He lives in Atherton, California with his wife, Joyce, and their three children.

Scuba Diving Safety is his third book. He also wrote **Medical Aspects of Sport Diving** (A.S. Barnes, 1970) and **The Old Fashioned Homemade Ice Cream Cookbook**, co-authored with Joyce Dueker (Bobbs-Merrill, 1974).

Fitness Books from
World Publications

The Complete Diet Guide: For Runners and Other Athletes from the Editors of *Runner's World*. How the athlete can use his diet to better advantage is the basis of this book. Areas addressed: Weight control, drinks, fasting, natural vs. processed food, vegetarian diets and more. Hardback $7.95, Paperback $4.95.

Living Longer and Better by Harold Elrick, M.D., James Crakes, Ph.D., and Sam Clarke, M.S. The authors believe that traditional medical practice has mistakenly concentrated on the treatment rather than the prevention of disease. This book stresses preventing disease through proper diet, exercise. Paperback $5.95.

Beginner's Running Guide by Hal Higdon. Everything a beginner needs to know to get started running on the right foot can be found in this book. The author draws on 30 years running experience to give you the most up to date and comprehensive knowledge in a breezy, personal style. Hardback $10.00.

Food For Fitness edited by George Beinhorn. A must for anyone concerned with protecting his health and increasing athletic performance. Answers all the important questions about diet and nutrition, do's and don't's of proper eating for all athletes. Also covers controversial nutritional practices. Paperback $3.95.

Complete Weight Training Book by Bill Reynolds. Improve your athletic performance, your posture, broaden your shoulders, reduce your hips—weight training can even help you lose or gain weight. Written by one of America's most famous weight training educators, there are workout schedules for 35 different sports. Paperback $4.95.

Basic Swimming Guide by Joseph K. Groscost. The *Basic Swimming Guide* has plenty of practical advice on teaching children how to swim. It deals with common problems in learning swimming strokes, and offers proven solutions. The book is oriented to children under ten years old. Paperback $2.50.

Available in fine bookstores and sport shops, or from:
WORLD PUBLICATIONS
Box 366, Dept. A, Mountain View, CA 94042.
Include $.45 shipping and handling for each title (maximum $2.25)